Presence in the Online World

Presence in the Online World

A Contemplative Perspective and Practice Guide for Educators

Edited by
Leslie Ann Jeffrey, Agnieszka (Aga) Palalas,
Karen Robert, and Yuk-Lin Renita Wong

ROWMAN & LITTLEFIELD
Lanham • Boulder • New York • London

Published by Rowman & Littlefield
An imprint of The Rowman & Littlefield Publishing Group, Inc.
4501 Forbes Boulevard, Suite 200, Lanham, Maryland 20706
www.rowman.com

86-90 Paul Street, London EC2A 4NE

Copyright © 2024 by Leslie Ann Jeffrey, Agnieszka (Aga) Palalas, Karen Robert, and Yuk-Lin Renita Wong

All rights reserved. No part of this book may be reproduced in any form or by any electronic or mechanical means, including information storage and retrieval systems, without written permission from the publisher, except by a reviewer who may quote passages in a review.

British Library Cataloguing in Publication Information Available

Library of Congress Cataloging-in-Publication Data Available

ISBN 978-1-4758-7025-1 (cloth) | ISBN 978-1-4758-7026-8 (paper) | ISBN 978-1-4758-7027-5 (epub)

Contents

	Introduction	vii
1	Guided Practice 1: Connecting to Land—Pause, Breathe *Bill Cohen and Karen Ragoonaden*	1
2	Being Whole in a Graduate Online Classroom: A Contemplative Perspective *Agnieszka (Aga) Palalas*	5
3	Cultivating Emotional Presence: Building and Nurturing an Online Community of Inquiry *Deborah Dell*	29
4	Vignette 1: Support for Contemplative Pedagogy through Shared Teaching Presence *Martha Cleveland-Innes*	49
5	Grounding Presence: Beholding the Vulnerability of Emergency Remote Teaching and Learning *Karen Robert*	55
6	Vignette 2: Presence and Silence in the Virtual Classroom *Margaret Anne Smith*	69
7	Connection and Compassion: Presence Inside and Outside the Online Classroom *Leslie Ann Jeffrey*	73
8	Guided Practice 2: Presence with/in/of Nature—Sit Spot Practice and Forest Therapy Walks *Monika Stelzl*	87

9 Fresh Eyes, Beginner's Mind: Contemplative Photography and a Walking-Based Pedagogy of Embodied Presence When the World Goes Online 93
Yuk-Lin Renita Wong

10 Hardwired for Presence in an Online World: A Contemplative Perspective and Practice Guide for Educators 111
Charles Scott, Heesoon Bai, and Laurie Anderson

Epilogue 131

Index 135

About the Authors 137

Introduction

Leslie Ann Jeffrey, Agnieszka (Aga) Palalas, Karen Robert, and Yuk-Lin Renita Wong

University educators find themselves facing accelerating and contradictory pressures as they seek to connect with their students in meaningful ways. On the one hand, the compounding crises of our age in the realms of public health, economics, politics, and the environment are wreaking havoc on our students' mental health and ability to learn. This climate of uncertainty calls for modes of deep learning that will help students develop a sense of meaning and purpose. At the same time, since the COVID-19-related lockdowns of 2020, many instructors, teachers, and faculty have been under pressure to adopt new teaching technologies and modalities for which they may feel ill prepared, especially if they have had little training in instructional design. Even institutions that once prided themselves on face-to-face instruction have been forced to adopt new methods of online or blended learning going forward.

The question addressed in this volume, therefore, is how we can bring the insights of contemplative pedagogy, which focuses on cultivating mindful presence, awareness, transformative growth, and deep connections in the classroom, into the space of online learning. If, as Parker Palmer, one of the early champions of contemplative education, has argued, "to teach is to create a space," then surely the online space, like the physical classroom, can be created in such a way as to enliven the spirit and heart as much as the mind.[1] The authors in this collection offer their reflections on their experiences in bringing the contemplative and the online together during these tumultuous years of emergency remote, blended, and online learning. In particular, they focus on the cultivation of "presence" in the online classroom.

"Presence," in this contemplative understanding, is a sense of "being there" in an open and holistic way, using modes of contemplative inquiry and practice (discussed below) to attune to all our inner and outer ways of being, and to become receptive to the moment unfolding in and around us. Understood through this contemplative lens, presence is about more than mere engagement or attention. Contemplative presence—this tuning in to both inner and outer worlds at a variety of levels (emotional, physical, intellectual, spiritual)—is what allows for the deepest experiences of learning and teaching as we move past our preconceived notions, attune to the possibilities, resonate with the experience of others, and inculcate growth and transformation at their most important level—the heart.[2] Contemplative presence acts as a spirit that can animate a deeply meaningful and transformative education.

Online teaching seems to fundamentally challenge the very possibility of such presence at many levels, because of the very real physical distance of online education, and because of the ways in which digital technology can play into distancing, distraction, and disconnection. Contemplative approaches require a focus and attentiveness, a slowing down and a "quiet," that can be very difficult to attain in our hyper-digital environments. David Levy has offered us excellent tools for becoming more "mindful" in our interactions with technology itself, more aware of and in control of our digital environment. But can we move even further into deep communication and communion with ourselves and others through and around this technology, in a way that cultivates openness, vulnerability, and connection with ourselves, as well as others?[3]

Experts in digital learning are at pains to point out that while online teaching brings with it well-known challenges, they are neither entirely unique nor insurmountable. Appropriate purposeful instructional design that cultivates community, self-regulation, and presence in online teaching can provide real educational benefits, including flexibility, increased access and inclusivity, and ultimately, broadened perspectives. The divide between "online" and "contemplative" may not, therefore, be as great as it would first appear. Indeed, contemplative and online/distance learning approaches do share some underlying affinities, including a concern for cultivating presence. Generally, however, these two pedagogical perspectives have not been in dialogue with each other. In this collection, therefore, we have brought together scholars from both of these fields to explore the possibilities for mutual enrichment. Thus, while it is important to acknowledge that most of us are not going to become experts in online teaching, we *will* continue to have to engage with technology in the postsecondary classroom, in some blended form, at least. In this collection we are sharing our stories of navigating in, through, and around the online environment. We argue that grounding ourselves in presence gives us a way to "tether" ourselves to ourselves and each other as we navigate the online landscape

We begin by unpacking some of our assumptions and understandings of online education and the possibility of fostering presence.

ONLINE LEARNING AND PRESENCE

While the past two years (2020–2022) were marked by an increase in conversation and research about online learning design and facilitation, arguably due to the COVID-19 pandemic and the emergency transition to remote teaching,[4] online learning in higher education has been mainstream for over twenty years, with leading academic institutions offering online learning courses in a variety of forms.[5] Online learning, which emerged after the World Wide Web was unveiled in 1991,[6] is a form of distance education that is managed fully or partially online.[7] With distance education tracing back to the eighteenth century, the application of online learning has been informed by over two centuries of practice and research of distance education pedagogy and over three decades of digital technology advancements. Online education has not developed as a substitute for face-to-face in-person learning, but rather as a unique educational approach with its own history, resulting in a solid theoretical and practical development.

Further, online learning, as a field of research and praxis, needs to be distinguished from the emergency remote teaching methods adopted during the COVID-19 pandemic. "Well-planned online learning experiences are meaningfully different from courses offered online in response to a crisis or disaster."[8] The differences between these two approaches to digital teaching and learning are vast.

The instructional design of online learning is carefully crafted with online faculty and students in mind so that appropriate strategies are employed to engage, facilitate, and assess students.[9] Traditionally, those who chose to and succeeded in studying online at a distance would be adult learners with higher levels of self-motivation, internal locus of control, and a need to study at a flexible time and place. They would be independent, place-bound, disciplined, goal-oriented self-starters, who "possess 'self' behaviors such as self-discipline, self-monitoring, self-initiative, and self-management, which are characteristics of self-regulated or self-directed learning."[10]

With the migration of our everyday communication and collaboration into virtual spaces, online learners today are usually fluent in the use of digital learning and communication technologies. They also have access to and value interaction and collaborative learning more than the previous generations of distance education students. The profile of the online learner has changed, "from one that is older, mostly employed, place-bound, goal-oriented, and intrinsically motivated, to one that is diverse, dynamic, tentative, younger, and responsive to rapid technological changes."[11]

As a result of this shift, the practice of self-study in traditional distance education and teacher-centered knowledge transmission, still common in face-to-face institutions, has been gradually replaced with student-centered learning based on knowledge construction through interaction in collaborative communities of learners.[12] Consequently, what originated as fully flex-time, flex-place, self-paced distance education has over time evolved into online courses that offer a balanced mix of asynchronous and synchronous learning. At the same time, fully self-paced asynchronous courses designed for higher levels of flexibility and independent study are also a significant part of the online learning ethos. These continue to require high levels of self-regulated and even self-directed learning.[13] Given the physical absence of an instructor, and often other students, the ability of learners to monitor and regulate their own learning is critical. They also should be able to create and manage their personal presence in the context of the course and take responsibility for their own success.

These characteristics of the online learner, along with pedagogical challenges and opportunities of the virtual learning context, have called for unique instructional design approaches that leverage and promote self-regulated learning. The online mode may reduce opportunities for interactions with other students and the instructor, and "as time is not typically structured around fixed instruction, online learners may need to provide their own structure around learning, determine for themselves when and how to engage with course content, manage their time efficiently, and persist in study despite competing life demands."[14]

Successful online instructional design thus requires the teacher to be present, involved, and supportive; their expertise and guidance needs to be carefully and seamlessly integrated into the course content, as well as its delivery, with the instructor almost invisible but always present. Facilitation, support, and scaffolding need to be embedded in the course design in ways that provide a clear path to learning for diverse students. For example, "flexible structure" that invites some "messiness" is essential to deep learning and growth. Carefully planned time together, rich in synchronous interaction, offers invaluable opportunities to develop a stronger community of learners, which is important to the overall success of online learners.[15]

Synchronous sessions can be an opportunity to engage in meaningful learner-centered activities that cannot be attained in the asynchronous mode, such as socio-emotional interaction fostering community building. The need for flexible personalized learning can be met by limiting the duration of such synchronous sessions and not planning activities that could be completed outside real-time events—for example, noninteractive lectures.

Thus, well-designed online learning pedagogical approaches rely on inquiry-based, exploratory, and dialogical learning, at times with elements of gamification for additional motivational support. Cohort-based online courses typically incorporate a variety of discussions and interactive and collaborative activities, along with self-paced individual assignments.[16] As mentioned, most online students select this modality for its flexibility, openness, and accessibility, so that they can engage in learning at the place and time of their choosing.

In short, the benefits of appropriately designed online learning have been proven across various educational and cultural settings. These benefits include, among others, flexible access to resources and instruction without physical and temporal barriers, and self-paced learning in an inclusive environment that provides guidance and facilitation. Online learning can also broaden and deepen educational resources by increasing access to multimedia learning materials and larger perspectives, and to diverse learning designs and learning resources, such as reading materials, videos, and worked examples.[17] In addition, it allows for customizable learning environments and multiple modalities of communication and collaboration.

In contrast, as an unplanned temporary delivery of instruction during a crisis, emergency remote teaching has different goals and expectations. It is a move from in-person instruction to a remote online method in response to an emergency.[18] Instructors who struggle with technology may not be able to obtain sufficient support to effectively navigate new pedagogical approaches and technology in the online environments and offer quality learning experience to their students.[19] In the context of emergency remote teaching, sufficient levels of online learning pedagogical and technological support, to both instructors and students, may not be available due to its provisionary nature and limited resources.

Consequently, instructors who rapidly switch to the online mode cannot offer the same level of preplanned, purposeful instructional design; engagement; or learner and teacher presence that are inevitably required for effective learning in a safe educational environment. This might be compounded by the challenges experienced by students who need time and intentional practice to develop the levels of motivation and self-regulation necessary to become successful online learners. As remote or blended modes of teaching have become more widely adopted, even in institutions that previously resisted them, it is essential to bear these differences in mind when discussing the opportunities and challenges of online learning versus emergency remote teaching.

The lack of physical presence and in-person communication, in both emergency remote teaching and online learning, may challenge structural and social aspects of learning, resulting in students experiencing disconnection, isolation, and boredom. Lack of motivation and meaningful involvement may lead to disengagement and even dropouts.[20] Some of the typical challenges of online learning that learners might experience, including feelings of isolation, inconsistent access, and technological challenges, as well as low self-efficacy and motivation, were exacerbated during the emergency remote teaching experience.[21]

Indeed, there are other challenges to "presence" that are inherent to the online context and its digital technology. Amplifying the transactional distance limitations, i.e., the perceived psychological, cognitive, and affective distances between learners and instructors in the digital space,[22] are the experiences of digital disarray marked by digital distraction, disorder, and disconnection.[23] Pegrum and Palalas submit that in the wider context of digital disorder characterized by the circulation of misinformation, disinformation, and fake news, another dimension of presence, namely "attentional presence," is essential to be able to separate substance from noise.[24]

Online learning actors' attention may be further challenged, among other potential distractors, by information overload, the abundance of choices, demands to operate numerous tools simultaneously, and to filter through a multiplicity of stimuli (e.g., video signals coming via Zoom), as well as built-in algorithms and persuasive design of digital technology that aims to capture our attention, often against our conscious will.[25] This leads to digital distraction, the lack of focus and concentrated attention so prevalent in today's attention economy.

Closely related, digital disconnection is experienced when digital learners are seemingly present online but, in actuality, are disconnected from the self, others, the content, and their surroundings. Paradoxically, online learners who tend to spend excessive screen time on their devices, supposedly connecting with others through social media, frequently feel disconnected from "real" people. They are plugged in yet tuned out, not present or engaged. They interact with digital personas, often projecting fake personalities. This undermines any sense of trust, connectedness, and relatedness that is the sine qua non of a healthy community of learners.

Recent research[26] further highlights the following challenges to presence experienced in online learning: the hyper-personal dimension of digital communication;[27] privacy and safety concerns that make the online space insecure; the feeling of isolation in the world of hyper-connection; mental health and burnout leading to avoidance/withdrawal; an ever-increasing pace, limiting engagement;[28] mental, emotional, and physical exhaustion and frustration, having to do more in less time due to all the various demands coming from professional and personal lives; and resultant increasing pressures on learners' self-regulation, time management, and connection to others, just to mention the most glaring issues which impact the online learning experience and the holistic wellness of the participants.

As mentioned above, to minimize the negative impact that these challenges may have on students' learning, online learning is designed to facilitate self-regulated learning, motivational strategies, and individual and community-based engagement,[29] as well as presence of both learners and instructors.[30] This is reflected in the key online learning concepts and design frameworks, one of the most prevalent of which is the Community of Inquiry framework, which follows the collaborative pedagogical principles aligned with the social constructivist theories of Vygotsky, Dewey, and Lipman.[31] With its focus on co-constructing knowledge in a shared learning space, the Community of Inquiry (CoI) framework "articulates three overlapping forms of human presence that coalesce to impact deep, meaningful learning through the development and sustenance of an online learning community."[32] The three kinds of presence include social, cognitive, and teaching presence (Garrison et al., 2000), which Dell describes in more detail in her chapter in this volume, and further proposes to add emotional presence to the framework.[33] Indeed, as Dell points out, there are a number of synergies between the CoI framework and contemplative approaches that can be productively developed.

However, while the CoI framework promotes meaningful learning through the development of an online learning community supported by three overlapping forms of presence (social, cognitive, and teaching—to which contributor Dell adds emotional presence, following few other scholars), it does not address presence through a holistic lens. We propose that online presence must include the learner's whole-person experience of inner and relational presence to self and others. Online education requires unique, deliberate, technological and pedagogical approaches that are purposely designed for the online ecosystem to promote the holistic well-being of learners, rather than merely cognitive "effectiveness." Students, more than ever, hunger for a sense of meaning, belonging, and deep connection, as their digital interactions—and often even their in-person ones—have been reduced to "fast-lane" transactional encounters. Contemplative approaches can help to foster that deep sense of meaning and connection to others and self that is so central to students' holistic well-being.

Thus, this volume aims to enrich online pedagogy's approach to presence with a contemplative perspective that treats the learner as a whole person who experiences physical sensations, feelings, thoughts, social relationships, and spiritual connections in relation to their own being and to their reciprocal and ethical relationships with others, across temporal, digital, and physical spaces. Our focus is on the learner experience of presence as opposed to solely the teaching presence concerned with design and facilitation, as "a means to an end to support and enhance social and cognitive presence for the purpose of realizing educational outcomes" (Garrison et al., 2000, p. 90; e.g., Garrison, 2016; Garrison & Vaughan, 2008). As Lehman and Conceição acknowledge the importance of the interplay of the inner world and the shared world, the experience of presence by "thinking, feeling, and behaving through interactions" results in "being there" and "being together."[34] The present volume expands this view by demonstrating how to foster connectedness in a contemplative space that promotes an open and receptive presence characterized by high levels of intentional attention and awareness. We propose that facilitating students' learning in the digital context goes beyond the social, cognitive, and teaching presences typically considered in the online learning design, to include contemplative presence—a "being there" holistically, to oneself and to others.[35]

CONTEMPLATIVE PRESENCE AND PEDAGOGY

At this juncture, as your consciousness is moving from the previous section to here, now, let's pause. Breathe fully . . . checking in as you arrive at this sentence, this word, this moment. How's the breath? What's the felt sense of the body as you are reading this question?

> Pause. Be the breath.
> How are you feeling?
> Pause. Be curious.
> What is reverberating in your mind consciousness? What are you anticipating reading in this section? How does this anticipation feel in the body? What's the felt sense?
> Pause. Be open.
> Where does the anticipation come from? What is it about?
> Pause. Be free.
> Can you be present to what is, without adding more commentaries?

To experience contemplative presence is to arrive afresh in this moment with our body-heart-mind-spirit being open to emerging possibilities that are not yet known. It is an "iterative and circular process of 'arriving' into presence, *beginning*, that is one of the preconditions of meditative awareness as educational enquiry. A moment when the Self itself may not have had the resources it needs to become performative, and intentionality, we might say, is still emergent."[36] As Scott et al. describe in their chapter in this volume, it is a moment of intersubjective presence when one brings into being the dialogic, turning toward another, not knowing where the meeting with the other will lead. It is a bodily intelligence, an "embodied cognition," distributed beyond the brain and encompassing the dynamic processes of the living body and the environment.[37]

What would the experience of teaching and learning look like with contemplative presence?

Since the mid-1990s, contemplative education has gained momentum in North American higher education. Academic initiatives like the Center for Contemplative Mind in Society (CMind) and its affiliated Association for Contemplative Mind in Higher Education (ACMHE) have brought together faculty from academic disciplines, including physics, medicine, law, political science, art, dance, literature, history, education, social work, and psychology, to explore ways of integrating spirituality and contemplative pedagogy into their course curricula.[38] This movement has also been fueled by feminists, racialized scholars, and Indigenous educators who have challenged dominant epistemological frameworks based on Eurocentric modernist knowing and objectivity.[39] Their work "opened the way for conceptualizing a curriculum of inclusion that drew from multiple views of reality."[40] To date, more networks or associations of contemplative education have been set up globally.[41]

Against the current consumer and technocratic culture in education, which treats knowledge as a consumer good, and privileges knowing through cognitive abstraction and distancing, contemplative education hopes to reestablish "sacredness as the ground of learning."[42] In *The Heart of Learning*, Glazer writes: "Sacredness is not understood within a particular religious framework but instead as growing out of two basic qualities of our experience: awareness and wholeness."[43] Awareness "is a natural, self-manifesting quality: it is our ability to perceive, experience, and know," which can be enhanced through attentiveness to bring a "greater sense of presence to the repercussions and meaning of our lives."[44] Wholeness "is the inherent, seamless, interdependent quality of the world."[45] In bringing the sacred into education, Glazer explains that the call to ethical behavior becomes stronger, not through code, law, or force, but through a direct meeting of the world with basic respect "where call and response—cause and effect—can be witnessed, experienced, understood."[46]

In *The Soul of Learning*, Keator and Watson further challenge us to bring the sacred into schooling with "radical vulnerability, authentic openings, and critical hope."[47] To do so, they remind us, we have to differentiate teaching as profession from teaching as transgression,[48] the institution of schooling from the nature of learning, and oppression from liberation. Citing W. E. B. Du Bois in 1903, "Education must not simply *teach work*, it must *teach life*,"[49] Keator and Watson ask: "What if the purpose of school is the learning of life itself? How would this change our orientation and direction?"[50]

Contemplative pedagogy cultivates awareness and presence to life within and around us through contemplative practices. Contemplative practices range widely: sitting meditation, walking meditation, mindfulness, centering prayer, *lectio divina* (holy reading), haiku, poetry, freewriting, silent time in nature, yoga, tai chi, qigong, aikido, contemplative arts, calligraphy, ikebana, contemplative photography, ceremonies, and many others. Central to contemplative practices is union of body, heart, mind, and spirit. Contemplative practice quiets one's mind, fosters a grounding centeredness to bring different aspects of oneself into focus, and restores wholeness. It nurtures one's relational presence to self and others (as discussed in many chapters in this volume) and awakens an appreciation of the interconnectedness of all life.[51] Through contemplative practice, one can develop a personal capacity for concentration and deep cognizance of one's mental habits, emotional tendencies, and preferences. Having developed an awareness of one's mental and emotional makeup, one looks deeper into their nature and engages in the kind of self-inquiry out of which arises the basis of wise action.[52] Thus, contemplative practice may shake up one's belief system and foster a social justice consciousness.[53]

Contemplative process is a critical first-person means of closely observing one's experiences, including the experience of thinking, and verifying the truth claim of third-person theories and concepts.[54] Simmer-Brown highlights the important subtlety of this point of recognizing the *experience* of thinking. So often we just habitually think and identify with our thoughts as who we are. Simmer-Brown asks: "Have we ever actually looked at a thought itself? . . . Have we turned our focus on critical thinking toward critical thinking itself?"[55] When we are aware and present to thought itself, we begin to recognize the difference between thinking and recognizing a thought, and the difference between thoughts and other kinds of experiences, such as our sensory awareness or emotional experiences. Learning to recognize thoughts as thoughts allows one to further inquire into thoughts, such as one's thought patterns, where it comes from, how it comes about, and what it does, rather than getting entangled in them. In this way, we can be aware and present even when thinking. This approach invigorates intellectual creativity and openness that is relieved from habitual thought patterns. It can also enliven a vitality and heart that is often lost in academic education.

The growing uptake of contemplative pedagogy in recent years, however, runs the danger of being co-opted for instrumentalist outcomes, such as attention or emotional regulation for higher productivity and better performance in educational settings plagued with neoliberalist and capitalist principles. As well, contemplative first-person learning which "turns the light of investigation inward"[56] to discover personal wisdom "through first-person discovery in personal experience and inner reflection along with traditions of research and third-person investigation"[57] can get appropriated to support the individualist stance separating us from our relations with others, and "our embeddedness in the biosphere, and our emplacement in the cosmos."[58]

Wary of the capitalist and neoliberalist co-optation of contemplative pedagogy and practices, Wong calls for "a more critical engagement of spiritual practices that are not of our own tradition . . . to maintain a critical pedagogy that refuses to allow the colonization of mindfulness into yet another Eurocentric and capitalist commodity."[59] Most importantly, it is to reassert the foundation of relational ethics in mindfulness practice. Kumar similarly invites us to go beyond taking contemplative practice, such as meditation and mindfulness-based activities, as methods or techniques to fit into the social and economic system. Instead, Kumar proposes viewing curriculum as a space for meditative inquiry to transform consciousness and to revitalize teaching and learning. He reminds us that meditative inquiry is not new, but has always existed. It is "our quest as human beings from time immemorial to ask fundamental questions about the meaning, origin, and purpose of life."[60]

Meditative inquiry can take many forms. It can be personal, as "a holistic way of connecting with oneself, a way to deepen awareness of one's actions, thoughts, and emotions" which are yet "never isolated from the people and world around us."[61] This echoes the Buddhist ontology of interbeing[62] and the theories of intersubjectivity, such as Buber's philosophy of I-thou relation.[63] As Scott et al. discuss in their chapter in this volume, "becoming a self is a relational process." Personal inquiry is thus necessarily "social and relational." In this sense, meditative inquiry is "the art of understanding oneself and one's relationship to people and the world . . . an art of becoming aware, an existential process of asking deep questions about life and our place in it."[64] It "helps us become aware of our fears and insecurities, an awareness of the way fears and insecurities cause greed, accumulation, and disparity."[65] Viewed from the perspective of meditative inquiry, education becomes less about information transmission or means-end learning but instead about "understanding ourselves in relation to each other ethically and compassionately."[66] Contemplative presence is thus always relational, to self and others, within and without.

That is, in engaging in contemplative practices to cultivate presence, we are laying the groundwork for a transformative education that seeks ethical and just relations based on compassion and love, and an embodied understanding of interbeing as respectively discussed in Jeffrey's and Wong's chapter in this volume. Contemplative education seeks to overcome the division and hierarchy that is often reproduced in mainstream forms of teaching.[67] It echoes and supports other critical pathways into new forms of knowing and being that are necessary for a better world to emerge. The "online" world of teaching and learning, rather than a necessary barrier to this emergence, can be creatively used to become another portal through (and around) which we can cultivate this sense of presence and connection.[68]

However, as noted above, the online environment and inappropriate learning design do carry risks of distancing and distraction. So, how do we develop a sense of presence, enable the capacity for openness, compassion, connection, and community, and create a safe space for vulnerability, curiosity, and growth to emerge in a potentially isolating and insecure world of online education? It is to these questions that the authors in this volume have turned their attention.

CONTRIBUTIONS

Working as an editorial collective, we value each of our contributions equally with our respective expertise and gifts. Our names as coeditors of this volume are ordered alphabetically. This is our embodiment of interbeing in coediting this volume from a contemplative perspective. In this collection we offer a reflection on the challenges and possibilities of cultivating contemplative presence in online teaching based on the authors' experiences of trying to bring contemplative and online pedagogies together during the years of emergency remote teaching brought about by the COVID-19 pandemic of the early 2020s. A year into the pandemic we organized a symposium, bringing together the authors in this volume to discuss our experiences. These chapters are the result of our continuing reflection on these discussions.

Contributors include academics from a broad range of disciplines and postsecondary institutions, some with a deep background in contemplative education, and others who had begun incorporating such practices just a few years before the COVID-19 outbreak. They range from digital learning experts to relative novices. Our diversity enriches this collective account of our experiences in creating and maintaining presence in the online classroom. Together, we reflect on our experiences over the past two years, sharing wisdom, success stories, and practices designed to foster connection and engagement in a digital space.

The collection combines longer reflective chapters with short vignettes that highlight classroom experiences and guided practices that foster a sense of shared presence in an online or blended teaching space. The volume thus offers readers a mix of conceptual wisdom, pedagogical theories, and practical tools. Our goal here is to inspire confidence in educators—to know that they can slow down and help their students resist the fractured attention of the digital world and build connection and community when they are learning together in an online space at a distance. The conversations range from theoretical and academic investigations of presence and education, including, importantly online education, to reflections on our experiences of bringing the online and the contemplative together during these years, to practical guides to adopting contemplative practices in, with, and around online technologies.

The volume begins with a land acknowledgment practice. Bill Cohen and Karen Ragoonaden walk us through some practices that literally "ground" us in the land where we find ourselves, even as we interact from a variety of physical spaces while online. Engaging in these practices in the online space, we become present to the history and the Indigenous peoples of the land, and "the multiplicity of intersections" that inform our sociocultural identity and all of our relations, past and present.

In the first section of the book, we bring together education scholars who reflect on the idea and practice of presence from the perspective of the online/distance educator. As we see in this section, "presence" is not a new concept for online/distance education experts; rather, there is a well-developed pedagogical discussion around presence which, although it may have different terminology and may not always play out in practice, does provide fertile ground for interweaving contemplative approaches.

Aga Palalas outlines for us the many ways in which she has been able to foster contemplative presence in a variety of "spaces" in the online classroom, i.e., in human-human, human-to-content, human-to-technology/environment, and human-to-self interaction. She emphasizes that key to enabling presence in the online classroom is the creation of a place of trust—a safe place free of distractions—and the "encouragement of a loving community" so that learners can interact "without hiding" behind the computer screen. As she illustrates through her own experiences, contemplative approaches can enrich distance education's understanding of presence by bringing in a holistic lens that moves beyond the cognitive and social elements of presence to embrace the intellectual, somatic, emotional, and spiritual dimensions.

Deborah Dell further builds on the particular role that mindfulness practices can play in resurfacing and encouraging emotional presence in the online classroom. As she notes, mindfulness approaches and online pedagogy, particularly in the form of a Community of Inquiry approach, which emphasizes co-construction of knowledge, share a number of productive overlaps that can be fruitfully conjoined.

Marti Cleveland-Innis's vignette on her experience of moving into distance education further enlightens us on distance education's understanding of teacher versus teaching presence—a more relational and interactive sense of presence. Again, this sense of presence as more than individual, and generated collectively between and among teachers and students, is echoed in contemplative understandings as we see in later chapters.

In the next section, scholars from a variety of disciplines who draw on contemplative approaches in their teaching share their experiences of bringing the online and contemplative worlds together during the years of emergency remote teaching. For the many of us who are educators but not well versed in either pedagogy—or, certainly, online pedagogy—the sudden shift was both frightening and overwhelming.

Karen Robert writes about how her contemplative practice enabled her to work not only with students, but with fellow faculty who were experiencing enormous amounts of stress and emotional upheaval during this time.

In another short vignette, Margaret Anne Smith shares her experience of being shocked and overwhelmed by the sudden shift to a virtual classroom. By coming back to her own capacity for mindfulness and awareness, however, she came to realize how a practice of allowing moments of silence to pause, reflect, or simply rest, which she had often used during in-person classes, could be similarly transformational in the synchronous online class.

In the following chapter, Leslie Jeffrey describes how she experimented with a variety of contemplative exercises during this period of emergency remote teaching. The practices were designed to help overcome the sense of disconnection from ourselves, each other, and the planet that seemed to be exacerbated by the digital classroom. Using a variety of exercises, including self-compassion, mindful nature walks, and loving-kindness practices, she and her students came to realize that presence, understood as a sense of connectedness and compassion, is a muscle that can be exercised whether one is in physical proximity with others or not.

Mindful nature walks were particularly powerful tools that allowed students to (re)connect with nature in this profoundly disconnected time. In the following guided practice, Monika Stelzl shares how she adapted forest therapy practices via technology during this time, enabling students to deepen their sense of connection to their own bodies, to nature, and to each other.

In the final section we bring in scholars with long roots in contemplative practice, leadership, and education. These chapters emphasize how establishing and maintaining presence requires nourishing an environment of openness to each other and creating a container that enables vulnerability. In this way presence can be fully manifested among and between us as teachers and students, as much as in us.

In her chapter, Yuk-Lin Renita Wong makes the case for creating a space for vulnerability, openness, and receptiveness as key aspects of presence that enhance students' capacity for connection with themselves and each other. For Wong, online presence is "less what we do with the technology and more about how we engage students in embodied practices that enhance their capacity to stay grounded and present, online and offline"—a critical capacity in developing the ability to engage with multiple viewpoints and diverse experiences in discussions of social justice. She outlines for us here a walking-based pedagogy that uses contemplative Miksang photography to help students tune in to their senses and cultivate embodied presence through preconceptual sight sensory awareness. In this way, along with the creation of a co-learning community in the online classroom, they practice maintaining an "open and receptive presence to what is challenging within and with each other."

Contemplative pedagogy forerunners Charles Scott, Heesoon Bai, and Laurie Anderson close this volume by reflecting on their experience of bringing their contemplative education classes online during the days of emergency remote teaching. Despite the challenges of distance and technology, both teachers and students learned to be present for each other in the online space. The authors remind us that "presence is a phenomenon inherent in who we are as conscious and aware beings," and it can therefore "be manifest in any ontic environment, whether virtual or face-to-face." Further, presence, in its fullest manifestation, requires both a deep awareness of the inner self and "dialogic engagement" with the Other. Such presence can be cultivated in ourselves as teachers and in our students through both inner work and "inter-work." By engaging in these practices, we can create the trusted "container"—that place for vulnerability and "loving community" that Palalas and Wong talk about. It is the creation of this space that encourages students and teachers to engage deeply and authentically and become our fullest human selves in both the online and offline worlds. Thus, with this final chapter we are reminded how the capacity to develop presence in ourselves as teachers and in our students depends not so much on the environment we find ourselves in, but the environment we create.

This edited volume is the first collection to bring a contemplative lens to the question of presence in the online learning space. Not only does this volume redefine the concept and experience of online presence, it also speaks to the significance of creating safe space and holding space for online learners so that they can be fully present and in presence with each other. The contributors provide examples of embodied online or offline practices. They discuss how these practices can enhance both the teachers and learners' ability to stay grounded, as well as regulate and co-regulate in the community of online learners. The collection offers a contemplative perspective that can potentially inform the universal design of online spaces to promote individual and collective learning. The contributors show how such nonthreatening spaces can be a fertile ground for new ideas, ways of knowing, and relationships. We hope that contemporary educators will benefit from the teaching and learning strategies shared in this volume that invite and celebrate learners' individuality, as well as engage with each other in their shared human condition.

NOTES

1. Parker Palmer, *The Courage to Teach: Exploring the Inner Landscape of a Teacher's Life*, 20th Anniversary Edition (San Francisco, CA: Jossey-Bass, 2017).

2. Mary Keator and Vajra Watson, *The Soul of Learning: Rituals of Awakening, Magnetic Pedagogy, and Living Justice* (New York: Routledge, 2021), 5.

3. David Levy, *Mindful Tech: How to Bring Balance to Our Digital Lives* (New Haven, CT: Yale University Press, 2016).

4. Aras Bozkurt, "From Distance Education to Open and Distance Learning: A Holistic Evaluation of History, Definitions, and Theories," in *Handbook of Research on Learning in the Age of Transhumanism*, ed. Serap Sisman-Ugur and Gulsun Kurubacak, 1st edition (Hershey, PA: IGI Global, 2019), 252–73.

5. Hope E. Kentnor, "Distance Education and the Evolution of Online Learning in the United States," *Curriculum and Teaching Dialogue* 17, no. 1–2 (2015): S21.

6. Ibid.

7. Tony Bates, "Online Learning for Beginners: 1. What Is Online Learning?" July 16, 2016, https://www.tonybates.ca/2016/07/15/online-learning-for-beginners-1-what-is-online-learning/.

8. Charles Hodges et al., "The Difference Between Emergency Remote Teaching and Online Learning," March 27, 2020, https://er.educause.edu/articles/2020/3/the-difference-between-emergency-remote-teaching-and-online-learning.

9. Bates, "Online Learning for Beginners."

10. Cheurprakobkit et al. (2002) as cited by Nada Dabbagh, "The Online Learner: Characteristics and Pedagogical Implications," *Contemporary Issues in Technology and Teacher Education* 7, no. 3 (2007): 217–26, http://www.learntechlib.org/primary/p/22904/.

11. Ibid.

12. Dianne Conrad and Jason Openo, *Assessment Strategies for Online Learning: Engagement and Authenticity*, Issues in Distance Education (Edmonton, Alberta: Athabasca University Press, 2018).

13. Ernesto Panadero, "A Review of Self-Regulated Learning: Six Models and Four Directions for Research," *Frontiers in Psychology* 8 (2017): 422, doi:10.3389/fpsyg.2017.00422.

14. Jaclyn Broadbent et al., "Technologies to Enhance Self-Regulated Learning in Online and Computer-Mediated Learning Environments," in *Handbook of Research in Educational Communications and Technology* (Cham, Switzerland: Springer, 2020), 38.

15. Dianne Conrad, "Building and Maintaining Community in Cohort-Based Online Learning," *Journal of Distance Education* 20, no. 1 (2005): 1–20; D. Randy Garrison, *E-Learning in the 21st Century: A Community of Inquiry Framework for Research and Practice*, Third edition. (Abingdon, Oxon: Routledge, 2016); Charlotte N. Gunawardena and Frank J. Zittle, "Social Presence as a Predictor of Satisfaction within a Computer-Mediated Conferencing Environment," *The American Journal of Distance Education* 11, no. 3 (1997): 8–26, doi:10.1080/08923649709526970; Linda M. Harasim, *Learning Networks: A Field Guide to Teaching and Learning Online* (Cambridge, MA: MIT Press, 1995).Third edition. (Abingdon, Oxon: Routledge, 2016

16. Another notable difference with emergency remote teaching is that with instructional designs following these purposeful theoretical and pedagogical guidelines in consultation with all stakeholders and in alignment with larger learning objectives, as well as program outcomes, online learning courses are usually developed over the course of six to nine months prior to initiation (Aguilera-Hermida, 2020; Hodges et al., 2020). At the macro level, online learning also benefits from dedicated IT department and Teaching & Learning Center resources trained in online learning pedagogy

and educational technology, as well as policies and systems supporting day-to-day online mode operations. As a result, online instructors/facilitators are comfortable in the virtual space that is structured carefully using selected educational technologies, e.g., Brightspace (https://www.d2l.com/), Moodle MLS (https://moodle.org/), Mahara ePortfolio System (https://mahara.org/), and Quizlet (https://quizlet.com)/. Both instructors and students choose online learning/teaching with clear expectations of its opportunities and restrictions, and hence are willing to invest the time and effort necessary to adapt to it.

17. Sabrina Ziebarth, Irene-Angelica Chounta, and H. Ulrich Hoppe, "Resource Access Patterns in Exam Preparation Activities," in *European Conference on Technology Enhanced Learning* (Cham, Switzerland: Springer, 2015), 497–502.

18. Saida Affouneh, Soheil Salha, and Zuheir Khlaif, "Designing Quality E-Learning Environments for Emergency Remote Teaching in Coronavirus Crisis," *Interdisciplinary Journal of Virtual Learning in Medical Sciences* (Online) 11, no. 2 (2020): 135–37, doi:10.30476/ijvlms.2020.86120.1033.\\uc0\\u8221.

19. Hodges et al., "The Difference Between Emergency Remote Teaching and Online Learning."

20. Mushtaq Hussain et al., "Student Engagement Predictions in an E-Learning System and Their Impact on Student Course Assessment Scores," *Computational Intelligence and Neuroscience* 2018 (2018): 6347186–21, doi:10.1155/2018/6347186.

21. A. Patricia Aguilera-Hermida, "College Students' Use and Acceptance of Emergency Online Learning Due to COVID-19," *International Journal of Educational Research Open* 1 (2020): 100011–100011, doi:10.1016/j.ijedro.2020.100011; Fernando Ferri, Patrizia Grifoni, and Tiziana Guzzo, "Online Learning and Emergency Remote Teaching: Opportunities and Challenges in Emergency Situations," *Societies* 10, no. 4 (2020): 86, doi:10.3390/soc10040086.\\uc0\\u8221.

22. Michael G. Moore, "The Theory of Transactional Distance," in *Handbook of Distance Education*, ed. Michael G. Moore, 3rd ed. (New York: Routledge, 2013), 84–103.

23. Mark Pegrum and Agnieszka Palalas, "Attentional Literacy as a New Literacy: Helping Students Deal with Digital Disarray," *Canadian Journal of Learning and Technology* 47, no. 2 (2021), doi:10.21432/cjlt28037.

24. Ibid.

25. Agnieszka Palalas, "Mindfulness in Mobile and Ubiquitous Learning: Harnessing the Power of Attention," in *Mobile and Ubiquitous Learning: An International Handbook*, ed. Shengquan Yu, Mohamed Ally, and Avgoustos Tsinakos, 1st edition (Singapore: Springer, 2018), 19–44; Pegrum and Palalas, "Attentional Literacy as a New Literacy."

26. Palalas, "Mindfulness in Mobile and Ubiquitous Learning: Harnessing the Power of Attention"; Agnieszka Palalas, "Mindfulness for Human-Centred Digital Learning," *Argentinian Journal of Applied Linguistics* 7, no. 2 (2019): 110–25; Agnieszka Palalas et al., "Mindfulness Practices in Online Learning: Supporting Learner Self-Regulation," *The Journal of Contemplative Inquiry* 7, no. 1 (December 31, 2020): 247–78, https://journal.contemplativeinquiry.org/index.php/joci/article/view/222.

27. Joseph B. Walther, "Selective Self-Presentation in Computer-Mediated Communication: Hyperpersonal Dimensions of Technology, Language, and Cognition," *Computers in Human Behavior* 23, no. 5 (2007): 2538–57, doi:10.1016/j.chb.2006.05.002.

28. David M. Levy, *Mindful Tech: How to Bring Balance to Our Digital Lives*, Reprint edition (Place of publication not identified: Yale University Press, 2017).

29. George D. Kuh, "What We're Learning about Student Engagement from NSSE: Benchmarks for Effective Educational Practices," *Change: The Magazine of Higher Learning* 35, no. 2 (March 1, 2003): 24–32, doi:10.1080/00091380309604090.

30. D. Randy Garrison, Terry Anderson, and Walter Archer, "Critical Inquiry in a Text-Based Environment: Computer Conferencing in Higher Education," *The Internet and Higher Education* 2, no. 2 (1999): 87–105, doi:10.1016/S1096-7516(00)00016-6.

31. Ibid.; D. Randy Garrison and Norman D. Vaughan, *Blended Learning in Higher Education: Framework, Principles, and Guidelines*, 1st edition (San Francisco, CA: Jossey-Bass, 2008); Norman Vaughan and Jessica Lee Wah, "The Community of Inquiry Framework: Future Practical Directions—Shared Metacognition," *International Journal of E-Learning & Distance Education* 35, no. 1 (2020): 1.

32. Deborah Dell, "Emotional Presence in Community of Inquiry: A Scoping Review and Delphi Study" (Athabasca University, 2021), https://dt.athabascau.ca/jspui/handle/10791/361.

33. Ibid.; Rosemary M. Lehman and Simone C. O. Conceição, *Creating a Sense of Presence in Online Teaching: How to "Be There" for Distance Learners*, 1st edition, Jossey-Bass Guides to Online Teaching and Learning (San Francisco, CA: Jossey-Bass, 2010); L. Susan Williams, "The Managed Heart: Adult Learners and Emotional Presence Online," *The Journal of Continuing Higher Education* 65, no. 2 (2017): 124–31, doi:10.1080/07377363.2017.1320204.1st ed., Jossey-Bass Guides to Online Teaching and Learning (San Francisco: Jossey-Bass, 2010

34. Lehman and Conceição, *Creating a Sense of Presence in Online Teaching*, 23.

35. Keator and Watson, *The Soul of Learning*; Parker J. Palmer, *To Know as We Are Known: Education as a Spiritual Journey* (San Francisco, CA: HarperSanFrancisco, 1993); John P. Miller, *Education and the Soul: Toward a Spiritual Curriculum* (Albany: SUNY Press, 2000); Mary Rose O'Reilley, *Radical Presence: Teaching as Contemplative Practice* (Portsmouth, NH: Heinemann, 1998); David Sable, "Reason in the Service of the Heart: The Impacts of Contemplative Practices on Critical Thinking," *The Journal of Contemplative Inquiry* 1 (2014): 1–22.

36. Italics in original. Tim Stephens, "A Meditative Enquiry into Presence: Unmaking the Autoethnographic Self," *Journal of Writing in Creative Practice* 14, no. 2 (2021): 176, doi:10.1386/jwcp_00020_1.

37. Francisco Varela, Evan Thompson, and Eleanor Rosch, *The Embodied Mind: Cognitive Science and Human Experience*, 2nd edition (Cambridge, MA: MIT Press, 2017); Yuk-Lin Renita Wong and Jana Vinsky, "Beyond Implicit Bias: Embodied Cognition, Mindfulness, and Critical Reflective Practice in Social Work," *Australian Social Work* 74, no. 2 (2021): 186–97, doi:10.1080/0312407X.2020.1850816.

38. See for example, Heesoon Bai, "Beyond the Educated Mind: Towards a Pedagogy of Mindfulness," in *Unfolding Bodymind: Exploring Possibility Through*

Education (Charlotte, VT: Foundation for Educational Renewal, 2001), 87–99; Daniel P. Barbezat and Mirabai Bush, *Contemplative Practices in Higher Education: Powerful Methods to Transform Teaching and Learning*, 1st edition (San Francisco, CA: Jossey-Bass, 2013); Kathryn Byrnes, Jane E. Dalton, and Elizabeth Hope Dorman, eds., *Cultivating a Culture of Learning: Contemplative Practices, Pedagogy, and Research in Education* (Lanham, MD: Rowman & Littlefield, 2017); Olen Gunnlaugson et al., eds., *Contemplative Learning and Inquiry across Disciplines*, Reprint edition (Albany: SUNY Press, 2015); Levy, *Mindful Tech*; John P. Miller, *The Holistic Curriculum*, 3rd edition (Toronto; Buffalo: University of Toronto Press, Scholarly Publishing Division, 2019); Sable, "Reason in the Service of the Heart: The Impacts of Contemplative Practices on Critical Thinking."

39. See for example, Nina Asher, "At the Interstices: Engaging Postcolonial and Feminist Perspectives for a Multicultural Education Pedagogy in the South," *Teachers College Record (1970)* 107, no. 5 (2005): 1079–1106, doi:10.1111/j.1467-9620.2005.00505.x; Gregory Cajete, *Look to the Mountain: An Ecology of Indigenous Education*, 1st edition (Durango, CO: Kivaki Press, 1993); George Dei, "Spiritual Knowing and Transformative Learning," in *Expanding the Boundaries of Transformative Learning: Essays on Theory and Praxis*, ed. E. O'Sullivan, Amish Morrell, and Mary Ann O'Connor, 2004th edition (New York: Palgrave Macmillan, 2002), 121–33; Fyre Jean Graveline, *Circle Works: Transforming Eurocentric Consciousness*, Illustrated edition (Halifax, Nova Scotia: Fernwood Publishing, 1998); bell hooks, *Teaching to Transgress: Education as the Practice of Freedom* (New York: Routledge, 1994); bell hooks, *Teaching Community: A Pedagogy of Hope* (New York: Routledge, 2003); Roxana Ng, "Toward an Embodied Pedagogy: Exploring Health and the Body through Chinese Medicine," in *Indigenous Knowledges in Global Contexts: Multiple Readings of Our Worlds*, ed. George J. Sefa Dei, Dorothy Goldin Rosenberg, and Budd L. Hall, 1st edition (Toronto; Buffalo: University of Toronto Press, 2000), 168–93; Riyad Shahjahan, "Reclaiming and Reconnecting to Our Spirituality in the Academy," *International Journal of Children's Spirituality* 9, no. 1 (2004): 81–95, doi:10.1080/1364436042000200843; Riyad Ahmed Shahjahan, Anne Wagner, and Njoki Nathani Wane, "Rekindling the Sacred: Toward a Decolonizing Pedagogy in Higher Education," *Journal of Thought* 44, no. 1–2 (2009): 59–75, doi:10.2307/jthought.44.1-2.59; Leanne Betasamosake Simpson, "Land as Pedagogy: Nishnaabeg Intelligence and Rebellious Transformation," *Decolonization: Indigeneity, Education & Society* 3, no. 3 (2014): 1–25, doi:https://jps.library.utoronto.ca/index.php/des/article/view/22170/17985; Yuk-Lin Renita Wong, "Knowing Through Discomfort: A Mindfulness-Based Critical Social Work Pedagogy," *Critical Social Work* 5, no. 1 (2004), doi:http://www1.uwindsor.ca/criticalsocialwork/knowing-through-discomfort-a-mindfulness-based-critical-social-work-pedagogy.no. 5 (2005).

40. Laura I. Rendón and Mark Nepo, *Sentipensante (Sensing/Thinking) Pedagogy: Educating for Wholeness, Social Justice and Liberation* (Sterling, VA: Stylus Publishing, 2008).

41. Some of these networks and associations include: Contemplative Pedagogy Network, Mindfulness and Contemplative Education, Mindful Society Global Institute, Mindfulness in Education Network, and Association for Mindfulness in Education.

42. Steven Glazer, ed., *The Heart of Learning: Spirituality in Education* (New York: Tarcher/Penguin, 1999), 10, https://www.wabashcenter.wabash.edu/scholarship/the-heart-of-learning-spirituality-in-education/.

43. Ibid., 10.

44. Ibid., 10.

45. Ibid., 10.

46. Ibid., 11.

47. Keator and Watson, *The Soul of Learning*, 4.

48. hooks, *Teaching to Transgress*.

49. Italics in original, Keator and Watson, *The Soul of Learning*, 5.

50. Ibid., 5.

51. Yuk-Lin Renita Wong, "Returning to Silence, Connecting to Wholeness: Contemplative Pedagogy for Critical Social Work Education," *Journal of Religion & Spirituality in Social Work: Social Thought* 32, no. 3 (July 1, 2013): 269–85, doi:10.1080/15426432.2013.801748.

52. Lata Mani, *Interleaves: Ruminations on Illness and Spiritual Life* (New Delhi: Yoda Press, 2011).

53. Rendón and Nepo, *Sentipensante (Sensing/Thinking) Pedagogy*.

54. Fran Grace, "Learning as a Path, Not a Goal: Contemplative Pedagogy—Its Principles and Practices," *Teaching Theology & Religion* 14, no. 2 (2011): 99–124, doi:10.1111/j.1467-9647.2011.00689.x.

55. Judith Simmer-Brown, "The Question Is the Answer: Naropa University's Contemplative Pedagogy," *Religion & Education* 36, no. 2 (2009): 94, doi:10.1080/15507394.2009.10012445.

56. Tom Coburn et al., "Contemplative Pedagogy: Frequently Asked Questions," *Teaching Theology & Religion* 14, no. 2 (April 2011): 173, doi:10.1111/j.1467-9647.2011.00695.x.no. 2 (April 2011

57. Simmer-Brown, "The Question Is the Answer," 93–94.

58. William F. Pinar, "Foreword," in *Engaging with Meditative Inquiry in Teaching, Learning, and Research: Realizing Transformative Potentials in Diverse Contexts*, ed. Ashwani Kumar (New York: Routledge, 2022), xii, doi:10.4324/9781003128441.

59. Yuk-Lin Renita Wong, "'Please Call Me by My True Names': The Decolonizing Pedagogy of Mindfulness and Interbeing in Critical Social Work Education," in *Sharing Breath: Embodied Learning and Decolonization*, ed. Sheila Batacharya and Yuk-Lin Renita Wong (Edmonton, Alberta: Athabasca University Press, 2018), 273, http://www.aupress.ca/index.php/books/120269.

60. Ashwani Kumar, ed., *Engaging with Meditative Inquiry in Teaching, Learning, and Research: Realizing Transformative Potentials in Diverse Contexts* (New York: Routledge, 2022), xix, doi:10.4324/9781003128441.

61. Ibid., xix.

62. Looking deeply into life and all existence, Thich Nhat Hanh observed: "To be is to inter-be." Thich Nhat Hanh gives an example of seeing a cloud and sunshine in a sheet of paper. He writes: "Without a cloud, there will be no rain; without rain, the trees cannot grow; and without trees, we cannot make paper." The cloud, sunshine,

trees, and the paper inter-are. Thich Nhat Hanh, *Peace Is Every Step: The Path of Mindfulness in Everyday Life* (New York: Bantam, 1992), 96.

63. Olen Gunnlaugson, "Establishing Second-Person Forms of Contemplative Education: An Inquiry into Four Conceptions of Intersubjectivity," *Integral Review* 5, no. 1 (2009): 25–50; Patricia Morgan, "Per-(Me-Thou)-Ability: Foundations of Intersubjective Experience in Contemplative Education," in *Contemplative Learning and Inquiry across Disciplines*, ed. Olen Gunnlaugson et al., Reprint edition (Albany: SUNY Press, 2015), 141–57.

64. Kumar, *Engaging With Meditative Inquiry in Teaching, Learning, and Research*, xix.

65. Ibid., xxii.

66. Ibid., xxii.

67. Heesoon Bai, Charles Scott, and Beatrice Donald, "Contemplative Pedagogy and Revitalization of Teacher Education," *Alberta Journal of Educational Research* 55, no. 3 (2009): 319–34.

68. Arundhati Roy, "The Pandemic Is a Portal," *Financial Times*, April 3, 2020, https://www.ft.com/content/10d8f5e8-74eb-11ea-95fe-fcd274e920ca.

BIBLIOGRAPHY

Affouneh, Saida , Soheil Salha, and Zuheir Khlaif. "Designing Quality E-Learning Environments for Emergency Remote Teaching in Coronavirus Crisis." *Interdisciplinary Journal of Virtual Learning in Medical Sciences* (Online) 11, no. 2 (2020): 135–37. doi:10.30476/ijvlms.2020.86120.1033.

Aguilera-Hermida, A. Patricia. "College Students' Use and Acceptance of Emergency Online Learning Due to COVID-19." *International Journal of Educational Research Open* 1 (2020): 100011–100011. doi:10.1016/j.ijedro.2020.100011.

Asher, Nina. "At the Interstices: Engaging Postcolonial and Feminist Perspectives for a Multicultural Education Pedagogy in the South." *Teachers College Record* (1970) 107, no. 5 (2005): 1079–1106. doi:10.1111/j.1467-9620.2005.00505.x.

Bai, Heesoon. "Beyond the Educated Mind: Towards a Pedagogy of Mindfulness." In *Unfolding Bodymind: Exploring Possibility Through Education*, 87–99. Charlotte, VT: Foundation for Educational Renewal, 2001.

Bai, Heesoon, Charles Scott, and Beatrice Donald. "Contemplative Pedagogy and Revitalization of Teacher Education." *Alberta Journal of Educational Research* 55, no. 3 (2009): 319–34.

Barbezat, Daniel P., and Mirabai Bush. *Contemplative Practices in Higher Education: Powerful Methods to Transform Teaching and Learning*. 1st edition. San Francisco, CA: Jossey-Bass, 2013.

Bates, Tony. "Online Learning for Beginners: 1. What Is Online Learning?" July 16, 2016. https://www.tonybates.ca/2016/07/15/online-learning-for-beginners-1-what-is-online-learning/.

Bozkurt, Aras. "From Distance Education to Open and Distance Learning: A Holistic Evaluation of History, Definitions, and Theories." In *Handbook of Research on Learning in the Age of Transhumanism*, edited by Serap Sisman-Ugur and Gulsun Kurubacak, 1st edition, 252–73. Hershey, PA: IGI Global, 2019.

Broadbent, Jaclyn, Ernesto Panadero, Jason M. Lodge, and Paula de Barba. "Technologies to Enhance Self-Regulated Learning in Online and Computer-Mediated Learning Environments." In *Handbook of Research in Educational Communications and Technology*, 37–52. Cham, Switzerland: Springer, 2020.

Byrnes, Kathryn, Jane E. Dalton, and Elizabeth Hope Dorman, eds. *Cultivating a Culture of Learning: Contemplative Practices, Pedagogy, and Research in Education*. Lanham, MD: Rowman & Littlefield, 2017.

Cajete, Gregory. *Look to the Mountain: An Ecology of Indigenous Education*. 1st edition. Durango, CO: Kivaki Press, 1993.

Coburn, Tom, Fran Grace, Anne Carolyn Klein, Louis Komjathy, Harold Roth, and Judith Simmer-Brown. "Contemplative Pedagogy: Frequently Asked Questions." *Teaching Theology & Religion* 14, no. 2 (April 2011): 167–74. doi:10.1111/j.1467-9647.2011.00695.x.

Conrad, Dianne. "Building and Maintaining Community in Cohort-Based Online Learning." *Journal of Distance Education* 20, no. 1 (2005): 1–20.

Conrad, Dianne, and Jason Openo. *Assessment Strategies for Online Learning: Engagement and Authenticity*. Edmonton, Alberta: Athabasca University Press, 2018.

Dabbagh, Nada. "The Online Learner: Characteristics and Pedagogical Implications." *Contemporary Issues in Technology and Teacher Education* 7, no. 3 (2007): 217–26. http://www.learntechlib.org/primary/p/22904/.

Dei, George. "Spiritual Knowing and Transformative Learning." In *Expanding the Boundaries of Transformative Learning: Essays on Theory and Praxis*, edited by E. O'Sullivan, Amish Morrell, and Mary Ann O'Connor, 2004th edition, 121–33. New York: Palgrave Macmillan, 2002.

Dell, Deborah. "Emotional Presence in Community of Inquiry: A Scoping Review and Delphi Study." Athabasca University, 2021. https://dt.athabascau.ca/jspui/handle/10791/361.

Ferri, Fernando, Patrizia Grifoni, and Tiziana Guzzo. "Online Learning and Emergency Remote Teaching: Opportunities and Challenges in Emergency Situations." *Societies* 10, no. 4 (2020): 86. doi:10.3390/soc10040086.

Garrison, D. Randy. *E-Learning in the 21st Century: A Community of Inquiry Framework for Research and Practice*. 3rd edition. Abingdon, Oxon: Routledge, 2016.

Garrison, D. Randy, Terry Anderson, and Walter Archer. "Critical Inquiry in a Text-Based Environment: Computer Conferencing in Higher Education." *The Internet and Higher Education* 2, no. 2 (1999): 87–105. doi:10.1016/S1096-7516(00)00016-6.

Garrison, D. Randy, and Norman D. Vaughan. *Blended Learning in Higher Education: Framework, Principles, and Guidelines*. 1st edition. San Francisco, CA: Jossey-Bass, 2008.

Glazer, Steven, ed. *The Heart of Learning: Spirituality in Education*. New York: Tarcher/Penguin, 1999. https://www.wabashcenter.wabash.edu/scholarship/the-heart-of-learning-spirituality-in-education/.

Grace, Fran. "Learning as a Path, Not a Goal: Contemplative Pedagogy—Its Principles and Practices." *Teaching Theology & Religion* 14, no. 2 (2011): 99–124. doi:10.1111/j.1467-9647.2011.00689.x.

Graveline, Fyre Jean. *Circle Works: Transforming Eurocentric Consciousness*. Illustrated edition. Halifax, Nova Scotia: Fernwood Publishing, 1998.

Gunawardena, Charlotte N., and Frank J. Zittle. "Social Presence as a Predictor of Satisfaction within a Computer-Mediated Conferencing Environment." *The American Journal of Distance Education* 11, no. 3 (1997): 8–26. doi:10.1080/08923649709526970.

Gunnlaugson, Olen. "Establishing Second-Person Forms of Contemplative Education: An Inquiry into Four Conceptions of Intersubjectivity." *Integral Review* 5, no. 1 (2009): 25–50.

Gunnlaugson, Olen, Edward W. Sarath, Charles Scott, and Heesoon Bai, eds. *Contemplative Learning and Inquiry across Disciplines*. Reprint edition. Albany: SUNY Press, 2015.

Hanh, Thich Nhat. *Peace Is Every Step: The Path of Mindfulness in Everyday Life*. New York: Bantam, 1992.

Harasim, Linda M. *Learning Networks: A Field Guide to Teaching and Learning Online*. Cambridge, MA: MIT Press, 1995.

Hodges, Charles, Stephanie Moore, Barb Lockee, Torrey Trust, and Aaron Bond. "The Difference Between Emergency Remote Teaching and Online Learning," March 27, 2020. https://er.educause.edu/articles/2020/3/the-difference-between-emergency-remote-teaching-and-online-learning.

hooks, bell. *Teaching Community: A Pedagogy of Hope*. New York: Routledge, 2003.

———. *Teaching to Transgress: Education as the Practice of Freedom*. New York: Routledge, 1994.

Hussain, Mushtaq, Wenhao Zhu, Wu Zhang, and Syed Muhammad Raza Abidi. "Student Engagement Predictions in an E-Learning System and Their Impact on Student Course Assessment Scores." *Computational Intelligence and Neuroscience* (2018): 6347186–21. doi:10.1155/2018/6347186.

Keator, Mary, and Vajra Watson. *The Soul of Learning: Rituals of Awakening, Magnetic Pedagogy, and Living Justice*. New York: Routledge, 2021.

Kentnor, Hope E. "Distance Education and the Evolution of Online Learning in the United States." *Curriculum and Teaching Dialogue* 17, no. 1–2 (2015): S21-.

Kuh, George D. "What We're Learning about Student Engagement from NSSE: Benchmarks for Effective Educational Practices." *Change: The Magazine of Higher Learning* 35, no. 2 (March 1, 2003): 24–32. doi:10.1080/00091380309604090.

Kumar, Ashwani, ed. *Engaging with Meditative Inquiry in Teaching, Learning, and Research: Realizing Transformative Potentials in Diverse Contexts*. New York: Routledge, 2022. doi:10.4324/9781003128441.

Lehman, Rosemary M., and Simone C. O. Conceição. *Creating a Sense of Presence in Online Teaching: How to "Be There" for Distance Learners*. 1st edition. Jossey-

Bass Guides to Online Teaching and Learning. San Francisco, CA: Jossey-Bass, 2010.

Levy, David M. *Mindful Tech: How to Bring Balance to Our Digital Lives*. Reprint edition. Place of publication not identified: Yale University Press, 2017.

Mani, Lata. *Interleaves: Ruminations on Illness and Spiritual Life*. New Delhi: Yoda Press, 2011.

Miller, John P. *Education and the Soul: Toward a Spiritual Curriculum*. Albany: SUNY Press, 2000.

———. *The Holistic Curriculum*. 3rd edition. Toronto; Buffalo: University of Toronto Press, Scholarly Publishing Division, 2019.

Moore, Michael G. "The Theory of Transactional Distance." In *Handbook of Distance Education*, edited by Michael G. Moore, 3rd edition, 84–103. New York: Routledge, 2013.

Morgan, Patricia. "Per-(Me-Thou)-Ability: Foundations of Intersubjective Experience in Contemplative Education." In *Contemplative Learning and Inquiry across Disciplines*, edited by Olen Gunnlaugson, Edward W. Sarath, Charles Scott, and Heesoon Bai. Reprint edition, 141–57. Albany: SUNY Press, 2015.

Ng, Roxana. "Toward an Embodied Pedagogy: Exploring Health and the Body through Chinese Medicine." In *Indigenous Knowledges in Global Contexts: Multiple Readings of Our Worlds*, edited by George J. Sefa Dei, Dorothy Goldin Rosenberg, and Budd L. Hall, 1st edition, 168–93. Toronto; Buffalo: University of Toronto Press, 2000.

O'Reilley, Mary Rose. *Radical Presence: Teaching as Contemplative Practice*. Portsmouth, NH: Heinemann, 1998.

Palalas, Agnieszka. "Mindfulness for Human-Centred Digital Learning." *Argentinian Journal of Applied Linguistics* 7, no. 2 (2019): 110–25.

———. "Mindfulness in Mobile and Ubiquitous Learning: Harnessing the Power of Attention." In *Mobile and Ubiquitous Learning: An International Handbook*, edited by Shengquan Yu, Mohamed Ally, and Avgoustos Tsinakos, 1st edition, 19–44. Singapore: Springer, 2018.

Palalas, Agnieszka, Anastasia Mavraki, Kokkoni Drampala, Anna Krassa, and Christina Karakanta. "Mindfulness Practices in Online Learning: Supporting Learner Self-Regulation." *The Journal of Contemplative Inquiry* 7, no. 1 (December 31, 2020): 247–78. https://journal.contemplativeinquiry.org/index.php/joci/article/view/222.

Palmer, Parker J. *To Know as We Are Known: Education as a Spiritual Journey*. San Francisco, CA: HarperSanFrancisco, 1993.

Panadero, Ernesto. "A Review of Self-Regulated Learning: Six Models and Four Directions for Research." *Frontiers in Psychology* 8 (2017): 422–422. doi:10.3389/fpsyg.2017.00422.

Pegrum, Mark, and Agnieszka Palalas. "Attentional Literacy as a New Literacy: Helping Students Deal with Digital Disarray." *Canadian Journal of Learning and Technology* 47, no. 2 (2021). doi:10.21432/cjlt28037.

Pinar, William F. "Foreword." In *Engaging with Meditative Inquiry in Teaching, Learning, and Research: Realizing Transformative Potentials in Diverse*

Contexts, edited by Ashwani Kumar, xii–xv. New York: Routledge, 2022. doi:10.4324/9781003128441.

Rendón, Laura I., and Mark Nepo. *Sentipensante (Sensing/Thinking) Pedagogy: Educating for Wholeness, Social Justice and Liberation*. Sterling, VA: Stylus Publishing, 2008.

Roy, Arundhati. "The Pandemic Is a Portal." *Financial Times*. April 3, 2020. https://www.ft.com/content/10d8f5e8-74eb-11ea-95fe-fcd274e920ca.

Sable, David. "Reason in the Service of the Heart: The Impacts of Contemplative Practices on Critical Thinking." *The Journal of Contemplative Inquiry* 1 (2014): 1–22.

Shahjahan, Riyad. "Reclaiming and Reconnecting to Our Spirituality in the Academy." *International Journal of Children's Spirituality* 9, no. 1 (2004): 81–95. doi:10.1080/1364436042000200843.

Shahjahan, Riyad Ahmed, Anne Wagner, and Njoki Nathani Wane. "Rekindling the Sacred: Toward a Decolonizing Pedagogy in Higher Education." *Journal of Thought* 44, no. 1–2 (2009): 59–75. doi:10.2307/jthought.44.1-2.59.

Simmer-Brown, Judith. "The Question Is the Answer: Naropa University's Contemplative Pedagogy." *Religion & Education* 36, no. 2 (2009): 88–101. doi:10.1080/15507394.2009.10012445.

Simpson, Leanne Betasamosake. "Land as Pedagogy: Nishnaabeg Intelligence and Rebellious Transformation." *Decolonization: Indigeneity, Education & Society* 3, no. 3 (2014): 1–25. doi:https://jps.library.utoronto.ca/index.php/des/article/view/22170/17985.

Stephens, Tim. "A Meditative Enquiry into Presence: Unmaking the Autoethnographic Self." *Journal of Writing in Creative Practice* 14, no. 2 (2021): 161–78. doi:10.1386/jwcp_00020_1.

Varela, Francisco, Evan Thompson, and Eleanor Rosch. *The Embodied Mind: Cognitive Science and Human Experience*. 2nd edition. Cambridge, MA: MIT Press, 2017.

Vaughan, Norman, and Jessica Lee Wah. "The Community of Inquiry Framework: Future Practical Directions—Shared Metacognition." *International Journal of E-Learning & Distance Education* 35, no. 1 (2020): 1–25.

Walther, Joseph B. "Selective Self-Presentation in Computer-Mediated Communication: Hyperpersonal Dimensions of Technology, Language, and Cognition." *Computers in Human Behavior* 23, no. 5 (2007): 2538–57. doi:10.1016/j.chb.2006.05.002.

Williams, L. Susan. "The Managed Heart: Adult Learners and Emotional Presence Online." *The Journal of Continuing Higher Education* 65, no. 2 (2017): 124–31. doi:10.1080/07377363.2017.1320204.

Wong, Yuk-Lin Renita. "Knowing Through Discomfort: A Mindfulness-Based Critical Social Work Pedagogy." *Critical Social Work* 5, no. 1 (2004). doi:http://www1.uwindsor.ca/criticalsocialwork/knowing-through-discomfort-a-mindfulness-based-critical-social-work-pedagogy.

———. "'Please Call Me by My True Names': The Decolonizing Pedagogy of Mindfulness and Interbeing in Critical Social Work Education." In *Sharing Breath: Embodied Learning and Decolonization*, edited by Sheila Batacharya and Yuk-Lin

Renita Wong. Edmonton, Alberta: Athabasca University Press, 2018. http://www.aupress.ca/index.php/books/120269.

———. "Returning to Silence, Connecting to Wholeness: Contemplative Pedagogy for Critical Social Work Education." *Journal of Religion & Spirituality in Social Work: Social Thought* 32, no. 3 (July 1, 2013): 269–85. doi:10.1080/15426432.2013.801748.

Wong, Yuk-Lin Renita, and Jana Vinsky. "Beyond Implicit Bias: Embodied Cognition, Mindfulness, and Critical Reflective Practice in Social Work." *Australian Social Work* 74, no. 2 (2021): 186–97. doi:10.1080/0312407X.2020.1850816.

Ziebarth, Sabrina, Irene-Angelica Chounta, and H. Ulrich Hoppe. "Resource Access Patterns in Exam Preparation Activities." In *European Conference on Technology Enhanced Learning*, 497–502. Cham, Switzerland: Springer, 2015.

Chapter One

Guided Practice 1
Connecting to Land—Pause, Breathe

Bill Cohen and Karen Ragoonaden

Like many other teacher education programs impacted by the COVID-19 pandemic, our campus rapidly pivoted to remote teaching and learning in March 2020. In June 2020, Bill and I adapted to an online delivery mode for a course on secular mindfulness. With close to 125 students, it was a challenge to create a learning community where shared experiences could inform sustainable practices.

We noted the particular challenge of articulating a land acknowledgment mediated by technology and separated by space, and, in some cases, time. To address this issue, we invited students to connect to the territory they inhabit by mindfully reflecting on their physical locations and the multiplicity of intersections that inform their sociocultural identity. The challenge was leading a large group of online students gathered in learning to consider the physical attributes of the lands they inhabit while reflecting on the diversity of languages, culture, ceremonies, and traditions of the First Peoples.

My colleague, Dr. Bill Cohen,[1] who leads many traditional Indigenous knowledge sessions informed by captikʷɬ stories, began our online course with these wise words about land acknowledgment.

> Syilx Peoples have been practicing land acknowledgments for millennia, a way of ritualizing place-based appreciation for gifts from the earth mother into our lives daily, from greetings to complex ceremonies such as the sniʔxʷám, or Winter Dance. The late chief, Barnett Allison, shared the following with me, which can be considered a morning greeting, prayer, land acknowledgment, a ritualized understanding. "The old ones made it through lots of hard times. Every morning before the sun comes up, they would greet all of creation with, 'waẏ kʷulncútn, kʷu ksx̌elpína? kʷu x̌ʷəlx̌ʷált!' We are coming alive with the new day and everything we need is here. Everything is possibility." Appreciation for diversity and inclusion ritualized into practice—made a part of our collective

everyday lives—means our collective intellectual and creative potential is much greater with women and Indigenous peoples contributing to the knowledge and wisdom our children have access to.[2]

Bill's words echoed in my mind as I adapted—and continue to adapt—mindfulness practices to support awareness and presence in online environments. Recognizing the caution against doing land acknowledgments as a formality, I reflected on how to connect the many strands of our practices to the respective territories where we live and work. I invite students to slow down and to pause. To sustain the development of recognizing presence, I use the practice below.

PAUSE PRACTICE[3] (3–5 MINUTES)

1. Stop.
2. Take three deep belly breaths.
3. Check in; see what is here now.
4. Be curious about what you notice without making judgments.

After the slowing down of the pause practice, I come back to the simplicity of a breathing practice focusing on gentle inhales and exhales. As an example, this breathing practice settles our thoughts and brings us to a place where we can, despite the isolation and technicality of an online environment, recognize the depth and breadth of the land acknowledgment by creating space to deepen gratitude, to reflect on our responsibility to the lands, and finally, to consider the importance of engaging in ethical relations with the human, and more than human, world.

BREATHING PRACTICE (10 MINUTES)

1. Find a comfortable sitting posture in your chair, on the ground, or, if you like, a standing posture. Let your hands rest comfortably, either in your lap or on your thighs; let your eyes gently close; feel your feet on the ground.
2. Begin with three deep breaths.
3. Bring attention to the sensations of expansion and contraction in the belly as you breathe.
4. Now, bring your attention to the sensations of the breath, moving freely in and out of the body.
5. Next, bring your right hand to your belly and your left hand over your heart. Notice if there are any emotions present. Simply notice.

6. Lastly, with each breath, notice any physical sensations in your body, areas where you feel tightness or discomfort. Just notice, don't judge; just let it be.
7. For the last few moments of this practice, I invite you to set an intention to embody a quality throughout the rest of your day. This quality might be kindness, generosity, curiosity, or presence.

After the pause and the breathing practices, I share a couple of Jon Kabat-Zinn's[4] seven attitudes outlining the foundation of mindfulness practices. I advise students to select a few attitudes that specifically connect and support their own online presence during the mindfulness practices.

- *Non-judgment.* Let go of judging and move toward non-judging. Come to realize how much of our time and energy is spent judging things, people, and situations.
- *Patience.* When we practice patience, we allow things to unfold at their own pace. We notice when the mind tries to rush things, and we allow ourselves to just be rather than frantically trying to hurry things along.
- *Beginner's mind.* With a beginner's mind, we approach each moment as if we are encountering everything for the first time. Rather than allowing preconceived ideas and judgments to determine how we react to a given moment, we remain open to new possibilities.
- *Trust.* Trust in yourself. When we trust ourselves fully, we do not ignore our feelings, our thoughts and sensations.
- *Non-striving.* We need to relinquish our tendency to strive toward a goal in exchange for a willingness to pay attention to whatever arises in each moment.
- *Acceptance.* Accept the present moment as it is. When we practice acceptance, we see things as they really are in each moment. We accept what we notice without trying to push things away or make them different.
- *Notice.* Notice, and then let go of, attachments. When we practice letting go, we just let things be as they are in the present moment, without grasping or pushing away.

Lastly, I show the image on page 4, which is the Chinese character for mindfulness represented by the ideogram of *now / being present* over the symbol of the *heart*. Using text or images, I invite each student to consider their mindfulness practices in relationship to the land acknowledgment done by Bill. I share that Bill's words remind me that as we cultivate the self to learn and to unlearn, the concept of now and being present supports the unfolding of time and space where the heart and mind converge in respectful and responsible ways of being and ways of doing.

BIBLIOGRAPHY

Cohen, Bill. Personal communication, 2022.
Cohen, Bill, and Natalie A. Chambers. "Emerging from the Whiteout: Colonization, Assimilation, Historical Erasure, and Okanagan-Syilx Resistance and Transforming Praxis in the Okanagan Valley." In *White Space: Race, Privilege, and Cultural Economies of the Okanagan Valley*, eds. Daniel J. Keyes and Luis L. M. Aguiar. Vancouver; Toronto: UBC Press, 2021.
Faculty of Education. SmartEducation Participant Booklet. Vancouver: University of British Columbia, 2015.
Kabat-Zinn, Jon. *Full Catastrophe Living: Using the Wisdom of Your Body and Mind to Face Stress, Pain, and Illness*, rev. ed. New York: Bantam, 2013.

NOTES

1. Bill Cohen and Natalie A. Chambers, "Emerging from the Whiteout: Colonization, Assimilation, Historical Erasure, and Okanagan-Syilx Resistance and Transforming Praxis in the Okanagan Valley," in *White Space: Race, Privilege, and Cultural Economies of the Okanagan Valley*, ed. Daniel J. Keyes and Luis L. M. Aguiar (Vancouver; Toronto: UBC Press, 2021).
2. Bill Cohen, personal communication, 2022.
3. Faculty of Education, *SmartEducation Participant Booklet* (Vancouver: University of British Columbia, 2015).
4. Jon Kabat-Zinn, *Full Catastrophe Living: Using the Wisdom of Your Body and Mind to Face Stress, Pain, and Illness*, rev. ed. (New York: Bantam, 2013).

Chapter Two

Being Whole in a Graduate Online Classroom
A Contemplative Perspective
Agnieszka (Aga) Palalas

One of the most profound realizations of my work as an educator and lifelong learner has been the significance of presence in the learning space—both the presence of individuals during their discrete learning experiences, and the presence of teachers and learners interacting in the process of knowledge co-creation. As a contemplative online learning practitioner, I have sought to create a digital classroom that invites the presence of my students and offers them my own presence as their guide and fellow explorer. In my teaching, I draw from constructivist learning theories that emphasize the collaborative nature of learning and co-construction of knowledge through social negotiation.[1] At the same time, I view each individual learner as a whole person who should access the wealth of their own knowing through the mind-body-spirit connection before they share it with others for collective inquiry. With the holistic experiential learning of individual students as the foundation, I encourage co-discovery of meaning through interaction and communication both in synchronous and asynchronous learning spaces. My perspective is that of a mindfulness practitioner who has explored, practiced, and taught open, digital, and distance education (ODDE) for over two decades, drawing on foundational ODDE theories (discussed in chapter 1 of this volume). It is through this lens that I share my experience and inquiries around presence and what it means to be present in an online learning environment.

Human-centered online learning requires intentional pedagogical and technological design as well as strategies that contribute to the holistic well-being of learners, rather than merely cognitive outcomes.[2] Learning is a lived, embodied experience that involves not only critical analysis but insights, feelings, and previous experiences, all of which are expressed mentally, emotionally, verbally, and somatically.[3] For me, learning is also a spiritual experience that connects the conscious and unconscious while integrating memory, will, intellect, emotions, and imagination.[4] With wholeness as a significant principle of my learning design, I strive to achieve balance between the intellectual, emotional, and spiritual dimension of being. I draw inspiration from the work of educator and author Parker Palmer, who observes: "Reduce teaching to intellect, and it becomes a cold abstraction; reduce it to emotions, and it becomes narcissistic; reduce it to the spiritual, and it loses its anchor to the world. Intellect, emotion, and spirit depend on one another for wholeness. They are interwoven in the human self and in education at its best."[5]

Wholeness goes beyond the individual to include the community of learners as well as the relationship connecting individuals to the broader society, planet, and cosmos.[6] It involves approaching "our students, teaching, lives, and all other forms of life with reverence,"[7] as well as love, compassion, humility, peace, and justice.[8] For the purpose of this discussion, however, I will focus on the presence of online learners in the here and now of their learning experience, synchronously and asynchronously. Before sharing my definition of presence in online learning, I will give a brief account of my mindfulness perspective.

MINDFULNESS IN ONLINE LEARNING

Through my decade-long applied research on mindfulness in online learning, I have observed and had a direct experience of the presence that can be manifested and enriched through the application of a contemplative perspective. Online learning requires thoughtfully designed teaching and learning strategies that take into consideration its distinct setting, learners, and technologies. The digital learning context, characterized by physical and temporal distance,[9] presents a myriad of challenges and opportunities for the sustenance of presence. While learning at a distance offers the pause and silence that invites reflection,[10] the instabilities of the digitally shared space, combined with the multifaceted channels of connection, have proven to be a persistent distraction to deep focused learning.[11]

Accordingly, I have explored the quality of attention as essential to presence in online education. I have been guided by Jon Kabat-Zinn's definition of mindfulness as "the awareness that arises by paying attention on purpose, in the present moment, and non-judgmentally,"[12] as well as Langer's understanding of mindfulness as "a state of mind that results from drawing novel distinctions, examining information from new perspectives, and being sensitive to context."[13] My colleague and I have recently proposed a working definition of attentional literacy that adapts traditional definitions of mindfulness to the specific context of our often alienating and disorienting knowledge economy,[14] where human interactions are mediated by technology. We define attentional literacy as the ability to intentionally direct one's attention, in the present moment, toward information originating from the self, others, and the environment (whether analog, digital, or blended), and to sustain that attention by choice, while remaining aware of and nonjudgmental toward new perspectives, multiple viewpoints, and shifting contexts.[15] This quality of attention requires an awareness of the full context in which learners participate, including their relationships with other learners and teachers, educational materials, technology, and space. Presence comes from attending to the dynamic interactions of these elements. Presence is being with all of these elements and being aware of that experience.

DEFINING PRESENCE IN ONLINE LEARNING

The definition of presence in online learning that I propose and explore in this chapter is the following: Presence in online learning is a holistic experience of purposeful interaction with self, others, content, technology, and/or surroundings, not necessarily all of them simultaneously, and awareness of that dynamic experience in the here and now of the online space.

To appreciate the uniqueness of online learning presence, it is essential to differentiate the online learner from learners who interact with others and with learning materials in person in the proximity of a shared physical space. Digital learners engage in their learning experiences from a distance, from wherever they are; they can connect with others through digital platforms either at the same time or with a delay; they can enter into a discussion through digital correspondence and explore learning content at their own pace. They might be "removed" by time and space but "connected" through a purposeful design that incorporates technology-based interaction between students, teachers, and content in multimodal environments (audio, video, and text).[16]

The online learners I describe here are graduate students of ODDE at an online university—Athabasca University. Most of them are practicing educators who have chosen to study online so that they can pursue their degree while continuing their professional career. They require the flexibility of online learning so they can attend to the multiple competing roles to which they are committed. While these students are mature and motivated, they are exceptionally busy and even distracted by these competing obligations. The students possess a strong academic self-concept and most of them exhibit an internal locus of control and self-directed learning skills. Though not all of them display high levels of self-efficacy and competency in the use of educational technologies, a majority have sound social learning skills, discursive or dialogical skills, and self and group evaluation as well as reflection skills, which are essential in online learning.[17]

Our graduate online classes are small (twelve to twenty-four students) and offer a mix of asynchronous and synchronous learning events and activities. The students are autonomous learners who are willing participants but also keen critics of their learning experiences. They expect the time and effort they invest to be highly relevant and effective. They are prepared to engage but equally quick to disengage, and they get diverted by the countless competing tasks that challenge their presence. Meaningful relationships with their learning and their cohort are essential for their successful learning experience.

PRESENCE IN ONLINE LEARNING INTERACTIONS

My definition of presence focuses on the learner's experience of purposeful interaction with self, others, content, technology, and/or surroundings. That experience helps the student to bring their whole self into the virtual learning encounter relationally, emotionally, cognitively, mentally, and spiritually by being fully in the moment through awareness and choice. In my students' cohort-based classroom, the quality of interactive connectedness is the pillar of learners' engagement and fulfillment. I refer to this dynamic process of copresence as human-to-human interaction.

PRESENCE IN HUMAN-TO-HUMAN INTERACTION

In our classroom, all of us are teachers and learners interacting in the dynamic discovery of knowledge. This interaction occurs as we collaborate, exchange resources, and communicate, using all our senses. The living process of human-to-human presence can be affected by the shifting states of self-awareness, awareness of others, and the motivation to connect in learning and to invest in that relationship. It requires intention and effort. Students show up for themselves and for others when they recognize their codependence and common goals in learning.

Their presence gains in strength when shared; it connects them when the human-to-human interaction is respected and reciprocated. Genuine relatedness and connection of teachers and learners to selves and to each other is essential to an online community of learners if they are to experience copresence. Learners want to connect with others because of their humanness and their story, because of the shared story; ultimately, it's the sense of oneness and belonging that matters to them. As teachers and learners, we have to invite our genuine selves—our essence, stripped of any digital persona disguise[18]—and hold space for all participants as we enter the circle with our stories and share our vulnerabilities with humility. Through practices of

ONLINE ADAPTATION OF THE "JUST LIKE ME" GUIDED MEDITATION

(Synchronous session adaptation: 5–10 minutes)
Invite students to keep their video on (only if they are comfortable with it) and to switch to the gallery view. Ask them to select one person in the video that they connect with through video.

SCRIPT

Begin by being aware that there is a person in front of you, that you are looking at in video (or in your mind, if you prefer). A fellow human being just like you. Silently repeat the following phrases while looking at your partner:

This person has a body and a mind, just like me.
This person has feelings, thoughts, and emotions, just like me.
This person has during his or her life experienced physical and emotional pain and suffering, just like me.
This person has at some point been sad, just like me.
This person has been disappointed in life, just like me.
This person has sometimes been angry, just like me.
This person has been hurt by others, just like me.
This person has felt unworthy or inadequate at times, just like me.
This person worries, just like me.
This person is frightened sometimes, just like me.
This person will die, just like me.
This person has longed for friendship, just like me.
This person is learning about life, just like me.
This person wants to be caring and kind to others, just like me.
This person wants to be content with what life has given, just like me.
This person wishes to be free from pain and suffering, just like me.
This person wishes to be happy, just like me.
This person wishes to be safe, strong, and healthy, just like me.
This person wishes to be loved, just like me.

Now, allow some wishes for well-being to arise:

I wish that you'll have the strength, resources, and social support to navigate the difficulties in your life with ease.
I wish that you'll be free from pain and suffering.
I wish that you'll be peaceful and happy.
I wish that you'll be loved because you are a fellow human being, just like me.

> Whether your partner is right in front of you, or you have brought your partner into your mind, thank that person for doing this practice with you. Give thanks in whatever way feels appropriate.
>
> *Thank you for doing this practice.*

compassion and connection on the basic human level, students can open up to their shared humanness and learner-to-learner interdependence.

One of the compassion practices I incorporate into my classes to experience our interconnectedness is my online adaptation of the "Just Like Me" guided meditation by Ram Dass and Mirabai Bush.[19] It invites learners to remember what we share as human beings and as learners/teachers.

Indeed, it can be difficult to relate to or reach out to someone when they're "closed off" for interactions and hiding behind the screen or carrying out their digital identity distant from their true self. By creating a safe, encouraging learning space that fosters social, emotional, spiritual, and intellectual "coming together," we invite the whole-person learner.

Synchronous Presence Experience in a Safe Virtual Space

Healthy learning communities rely on a mutual sense of connectedness and relatedness. Unfortunately, digital spaces are plagued with challenges of distraction, disconnection, and other digital well-being threats (such as cyberbullying, fake digital identity, digital drama, etc.) that, if not addressed, can undermine these relational foundations. It is thus essential to create safe online learning spaces that are built on trust. The following online learning event exemplifies how I used purposeful learning design and ad hoc teaching strategies to offer the experience of safety and trust in my synchronous graduate class.

Synchronous sessions offer a precious time together that should encourage direct connection and communication which is fundamental to the cohort human-to-human interaction (Hoven et al., 2020). The cohort-based course design supports self-regulation and co-regulation that further motivates self-directed learning and continuity of engagement that links the synchronous and asynchronous spaces (connection spanning same-time and self-paced learning events/episodes of the course). To create a safe, nonthreatening, and empowering learning environment, we start by negotiating the time and space boundaries for the course to respect students' diverse needs and preferences. Through a dedicated online forum and discussion, I guide them to raise their awareness of the various aspects of digital disarray. An experiential practice follows that invites the students to monitor their digital habits (e.g., cellphone practice; digital journal) and subsequently to cultivate healthy digital habits, including a regular digital detox practice (e.g., agreeing on a day a week that we are not expected to use our digital devices, including for coursework). Together, we identify digital well-being safety guidelines for our class, which incorporate digital awareness and relationship contract.

To create a real-time experience conducive to high levels of moment-to-moment presence, I encourage learners to also declutter their synchronous spaces to avoid any distractors and distancers. For example, as students engage in their arrival breathing practice, I invite them to close any additional digital platforms or devices and, at the same time, to feel safe in their physical surroundings (e.g., their room, office, garden). I also invite them to declutter their inner space through a brief body scan or a similar mindfulness moment. While engaged in arrival and breathing practices, I ensure that students feel grounded and attend to their present experience.

In my invitations to connect with their real experiences, I acknowledge students' diverse circumstances and mindsets. I pay attention to their verbal and bodily expressions so that I can attune to their experiences and respect their varying levels of engagement and comfort, which is not always without challenges in the online space. We use centering practices, usually with students' cameras turned off, to help them "arrive" and get grounded while leaving their other demands at the virtual entrance. Students type in the chat "I have

MINDFUL LISTENING MEDITATION

DEEP LISTENING

(Synchronous session adaptation; 10–15 minutes)
Students are put into breakout rooms in pairs. Invite students to keep their video on (only if they are comfortable). Then, one person speaks and the other listens in complete silence. The listener listens as carefully as possible, letting go of interpretations, judgments, and reactions, as well as irrelevant thoughts, memories, and plans. When the speaker finishes, the listener repeats as closely as possible what the speaker said. The original speaker sits in silence while the listener repeats this back to them.

STEP-BY-STEP INSTRUCTIONS FOR STUDENTS

1. Take turns listening and speaking.
2. One partner will spend three minutes speaking about a course topic or an aspect of their life. Set a timer that will make a noise when the three minutes is up, avoiding looking at the time.

3. These three minutes are devoted to the speaker. The listener sits in silence. If the speaker runs out of things to say, sit in silence. Whenever you have something to say, you may continue speaking again.
4. The listener should listen in silence. When you listen, give your full attention to the speaker. Be curious, but don't ask questions while listening. You may acknowledge with facial expressions or by nodding your head. Try not to over-acknowledge. You may feel an urge to coach, identify, chime in, or interrupt. This is normal. Just notice when this occurs and resist the temptation to act. Listen with kindness. When thoughts or emotions come into your mind, simply notice them and gently return your full attention to the speaker. If the speaker runs out of things to say, give them the space for silence, and then be available to listen when they speak again.
5. After the alarm sounds, set the alarm for one minute.
6. Repeat what you have heard from the speaker. Simply paraphrase, don't memorize.
7. After the alarm sounds, the speaker should take one more minute to clarify anything they feel was misunderstood by the listener. Again, one person speaks at a time in a kind and respectful manner.
8. Switch roles. Now the speaker is the listener and the listener the speaker. Repeat steps one through four.
9. Reflect on how it feels to be listened to so closely and what it felt like to listen deeply to another person. This can be a conversation lasting however long you prefer.
10. End by thanking the other person for listening.

Thank you for doing this practice.

arrived," "I'm here now," I'm ready," and other synonymous phrases, once they feel present and ready to interact. This is the right moment to also invite students to share their personal revelations and aha moments during our session check-ins. Students observe that they find these exchanges fundamental to building mutual trust.

To further encourage trust and openness, I incorporate a mindful listening meditation followed by a debrief and discussion of deep listening strategies. This is preceded by a padlet / Post-it activity where students share anonymously their special talents and experiences which highlights the collective expertise and resourcefulness of the educators in the virtual room.

I have observed that when students practice mindful listening during our collective inquiry into their lived experiences of digital learning/ teaching, they offer their genuine insights without fear of being "wrong" or "exposed." They share their unique voices and feel safe to experiment with their thoughts and guesses.

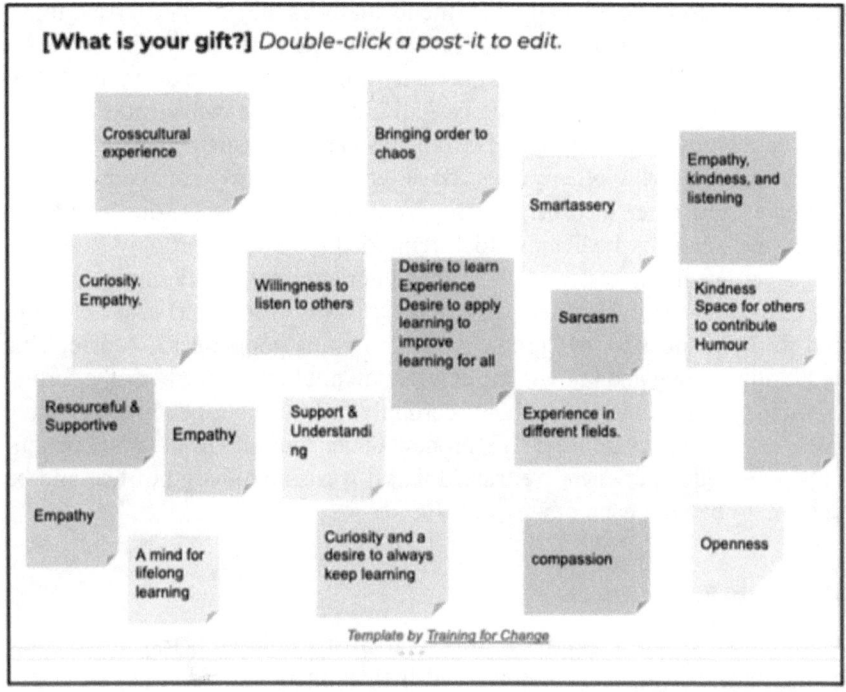

Figure 2.3. Padlet/Post-it Activity. *Source*: Adapted by Aga Palalas from Training for Change Template at https://www.trainingforchange.org/tools

Trust Invites Human-to-Human Interaction

In one such synchronous session, after the mindful listening exercise, a student commented that she felt more comfortable sharing her own perspective knowing that her classmates were listening for "her meaning" rather than for the "correct" answer. Having a forum where her voice and story were honoured enabled her to trust her own knowing and that of others. That explicit declaration of trust set up the tone for the session.

Students chose to have their videos on (which I always encourage, but leave up to the participants, as their mental, physical, and technological circumstances differ). Their attention was evidently on the conversation, regardless of the physical and virtual space distractors that I could still hear coming in the form of audio notifications. Students were *on*, offering their undivided attention, as well as their less "censored" questions, observations, and feelings. They seemed to fully disregard any potential physical, technological, or "hierarchical" distance, and subsequently reported not feeling isolated but rather being connected in the real-time virtual space. They commented on their experience of belonging in that exchange of energy and space in which they were present emotionally and intellectually as they connected and tuned in to a degree that made them feel safe and relevant.

With the session learning goal gradually transforming into a genuine heartfelt intention to share and belong, we all indulged in a conversation that redefined the meaning of right and wrong answers. We were then fully open to listening and hearing other perspectives, witnessing new ideas coming from ourselves and other members of the group during that vigorous exchange. When the timer on the Teams clock reminded the group that only five minutes were left in the session, we switched our attention to the session agenda with its to-do list, which seemed to pull us away from the present moment and shift our focus to the "premeditated" learning goals for the course. This symbiotic sharing and knowledge co-creation might not have been the formal learning goal for the session, but it certainly followed our genuine collective intention to interact in order to gain new understanding. In the nonthreatening connected experience, we trusted that it was safe to let go of fear and be present, to be with each other.

Vulnerability Connects

Letting go and not being afraid that their trust would be betrayed, students could connect with their feelings and their vulnerabilities—a key to establishing and maintaining presence in the online classroom. Vulnerability can connect and engage all of us in the shared learning space. This was vividly manifested when my Indigenous colleague was invited, as our guest speaker, to present on Indigenous research and pedagogy in a synchronous session. By this point of the semester, students were all accustomed to our routine Teams session structure that would start with an arrival practice and incorporate debriefing, mindful listening and speaking practices, as well as reflection-based learning activities. Students trusted each other and felt safe with the group and with me, their instructor/guide. They were introduced to contemplative pedagogy and encouraged to apply a holistic lens in their exploration of online learning theory and praxis, which was the focus of the course. Students explicitly articulated their shared intention for the session: to actively interact and allow themselves to be and feel whatever came up; to be open and curious; and to appreciate the holistic approach to research and pedagogy as presented by my Indigenous colleague. Students were prepared for the session through a prior exploration of the topic.

Nine of the ten students, guest speaker, and I kept our cameras on to foster higher levels of bodily connection with the guest and colleagues. The guest speaker invited us to focus in our check-ins on who we felt we were as people (not professionals), identifying our roots and how we belonged to our communities. As students spoke, I felt that some of them wanted to let us in—they wanted to "get closer"—whereas others were "playing it safe." When my turn came and I spoke of my Polish roots and family in Poland, I felt my emotions come up. I experienced even deeper levels of presence as I shed some tears of nostalgia. Students who witnessed my vulnerability reported later that they felt exceptionally close to me at that point; I also sensed their presence more than ever before. They sent me emails and messages of love when I became emotional. One of them cited Maya Angelou: "We can learn to see each other and see ourselves in each other and recognize that human beings are more alike than unalike."

Another student acknowledged my vulnerability and my presence by typing in the Teams chat: "I see you, Dr. Aga." I felt even more connected as their peer and fellow being. When my emotions boiled up, students were able to hold space for me with warmth and compassion. Their subsequent comments indicated that students connected to the Indigenous scholar at a deep level as well. They opened up and welcomed her authentic self and her knowledge perspective. They felt respected as humans in that conversation that focused on respect, relevance, reciprocity, and responsibility, with emphasis on one's connection to their land and belonging; her spirituality and submission to a higher "collective being" was felt and explicitly expressed.

PRESENCE IN HUMAN–CONTENT INTERACTION

While the sense of community and various forms of human–human interactivity are indispensable to successful online learning,[20] ODDE researchers and practitioners have all along agreed on the significance of the learner–content interaction;[21] some even posited that learner–content interaction is "the fundamental form of interaction on which all education is based."[22] For learners to purposefully engage with content, both that which they "consume" and that which they "produce," and to pay attention to it out of choice, they need to feel that the message in the content is relevant to them—that it speaks to them on one level or another. To offer that meaningful experience, learning content and its delivery require intentional pedagogical design that invites this connection and reflection. With asynchronous resources being prerecorded and documented, they are not as agile as those in synchronous interactions; hence, creating learning content that engenders the experience of presence necessitates planning and authenticity. Thoughtful asynchronous design and teaching/facilitation begin with the instructor's own sense of presence.

I also foster a sense of community through student engagement with learning content—a myriad of multimedia artifacts that might include learner cocreated videos, blogs, and websites. Students connect by sharing these artifacts and exchanging posts, notes, videos, or photos. Discussion forums represent one of the most common strategies to promote asynchronous presence through content. Forums might employ scenario-based discussion strategies, including structured, scaffolded, debate, and role-play approaches.[23] Other potential channels of student–student and student–teacher exchange include email, chat, blogs, YouTube, TikTok, etc.

The authenticity and reciprocity typically observed in synchronous communication can also be approximated in delayed interactions. These exchanges, by their asynchronous nature, offer silence and a pause in time conducive to deeper reflection before action or reflection in action.[24] They invite presence when participants create content and also when they attend to content created by others. Students and teachers can be present *in* the course content when they express themselves in their creations for subsequent asynchronous interaction. They can also be present *with* that content when they discover the meaning expressed through content authored by others synchronously. Presence can thus be captured and experienced in the human–content interaction.

Asynchronous Presence *in* Content

One's presence to a moment that is captured and recorded in a learning artifact can be an invitation for others to witness or to join in the co-creation of knowledge if they are open and ready to partake. Authors can be present *in* content when they are ready to convey what comes up for them. For students, engagement in self-inquiry may result in student-generated pieces that exude meaning, relevance, and mind-body-spirit knowing. These highly introspective and communicative discussion posts, assignments, emails, photos, or presentations can be created by students individually and collectively when they feel listened to, safe, and respected. They can be present in the asynchronously crafted piece on their own time when they feel ready to give it attention and motivated to give it effort. I consistently use messages of support, gratitude, and compassion to help my students center and recognize the brilliant contributions they have to offer to their own learning journey and that of their peers, always reminding them that everybody in the room is a teacher and a learner, and they all contribute their invaluable diverse perspectives.

Mindful feedback is a strategy that motivates my students to express their authentic ideas and feelings in their work. I offer asynchronous feedback in the form of inquiries to stimulate reflection. Using appreciative language, I acknowledge students' insights, feelings, and ideas with special emphasis given to those that are unique to their standpoint or circumstances. I pose questions for reflection to encourage learners' deeper contemplation and openness. For example, I might write in my comments: "Read this sentence again; close your eyes and sit with it; witness what comes up; share any new insights in your reply to my comment."

To encourage students to revisit an idea from the beginner's mind perspective, I ask them to drop their preconceptions: "If you had never studied XYZ, how would you explain scaffolding (surprise me :-))?" I invite students to lean into their shifting ideas with curiosity for new understandings, treating errors and omissions as opportunities for deeper self-inquiry so that they can balance their conceptual, analytical, and social understanding with self-awareness. The explicit intention of my comments is to invite deeper reflection engendered by the whole-person connection with the self and the content. Students and I enter into an asynchronous conversation through replies to comments that often prompt them to resubmit their work to better represent themselves. When the author infuses the content with authentic presence in the moment of creation, that presence can be experienced in the resulting learning artifacts. The author's presence is captured in the learning content they create.

Asynchronous Presence *with* Content

The author's presence subsequently invites the receiver's presence. While I don't necessarily engage with mechanically written research reports following a template, the students' own reflections usually pull me into their rich world of knowing. Similarly, students enthusiastically interact with content that is authentic and meaningful to them. They intuitively connect with course materials, as well as resources created by their peers that touch them at a deeper level, surpassing their cognitive curiosity.

The experience of presence might be brought about through something as simple as a smiley icon or a picture in the chat box, audio and written teacher's comments that make the message relevant to the whole person's sense of purpose. It could be another student posting the same question they have on their mind, a video that inspires their aha moment, or a classmate's call for assistance. Recorded language and symbols allow us to communicate across time and physical distances, bringing past experiences, stories, and thoughts into the here and now. Learners can be fully engaged with their mind-body-spirit when interacting with a message, sensation, or relationship conveyed by the authors; they can also enter, on purpose in the present moment, into a deeply engaging interaction with the meaning they discover in that content for themselves.

Students can be present *with* content when they are invited to query it, contemplate on it, and find their meaning in it. They can also be co-present with content when engaged in a knowledge co-construction circle, especially when they are invited to an inquiry-based discussion in which diverse views are encouraged rather than judged. I use images of tapestry to motivate students to weave their threads into the colorful asynchronous discussion one post at a time, whenever they are ready. Linking their pieces with those of others can be explicit but also tacit, especially for those learners who "lurk" in the background in discussion forums and often come alive in individual assignments, such as reflective journals. Below I describe an example of such an assignment that, in my practice, has demonstrated online learners' asynchronous presence most overtly.

Reflective Journals

Students in all my courses are expected to write journals and share portions of their reflections with me. We spend time discussing the meaning of reflection based on relevant publications, starting with a book by Ellen Rose, *On Reflection: An Essay on Technology, Education, and the Status of Thought in the 21st Century*.[25] Students subsequently share with me examples of their journal posts and I offer mindful feedback by incorporating prompts and questions. I encourage students to set, and reset, intentions for their journals and to incorporate creative artifacts as they contemplate their learning journey. I award full marks for the journals to shift the attention to the process and away from the product. In this internal inquiry practice, students often connect with their self-understanding and humbly open up, filling in some "blanks" and sharing their "unspoken" words—their authentic experiences, questions, doubts, revelations, emotions, and hopes. Their presence is evident in the content of their journals. I feel honored to be able to witness their journey, which I express to them in my feedback.

Often when I interact with the content shared by students—with no rush, no interruptions—delectating in the students' words on my screen, I find myself talking to them. When their posts and sharings invite my deep deliberation, I ask a question or share a comment as if I were in conversation with them—I am present *with* their journals and interact with students *in* my delayed feedback. Other times, I just "listen" to the words on the screen and nod my head. Being present with their message, I would pause in silence or reread their words like a mantra. Other times, I don't connect with their writing on any level other than cognitive; I do not find their whole selves in their work.

PRESENCE IN INTERACTION WITH THE SELF

The learner's interaction with the self is fundamental to all other dimensions of interaction in online learning, though it is rarely discussed by ODDE researchers (e.g., Soo & Bonk, 1998). The interaction with the self that I encourage in my online classroom transcends the ODDE perspective that focuses on "the learner's reflections on the content, learning process and . . . new understanding"[26] as the meta-cognitive processes that help students to regulate and structure their learning.[27] While this aspect of learner self-regulation is imperative in online learning, it is the contemplative dimension of self-inquiry that enables learners to become more intimate with the subject they explore. That connection with the inner self is the first step on the pathway toward education that promotes growth and evolution of knowledge.

To encourage contemplative self-inquiry, I introduce readings about openness, growth, vulnerability, contradiction, and attention, as well as self-love and love for others. In the welcome message of my course, I often share the poem "Everything Is Waiting for You," by David Whyte.[28] Afterward, I invite students to share their personal notes, pictures, poems, phrases, or any other artifacts that express who they are and what matters to them as they start on this learning journey. At the initial stages of the course, only a few students are ready to show up and be present as human beings; they tend to be more comfortable in their roles as educators and graduate students. Through the subsequent discussion, I prompt them to rethink the learning they are seeking. I introduce the practice of first-person, subjective inquiry that begins with a here-and-now whole-learner experience, starting with a version of the breath or body scan exercise.[29]

I also include reminders to pause and reconnect with the self in my synchronous and asynchronous learning tasks. Later in the course, I invite students to reflect on their interactions with the subject matter and their own teaching and educational leadership practices. For instance, when students design solutions as part of the educational leadership case studies, I encourage them to sit with those challenging cases and jot down in their journals what emotions they feel when they consider socioeconomic educational problems. I also invite them to reflect on how their reactions connect to their values, to examine the case study through a personal lens and become aware of what they are experiencing.

That self-understanding better prepares them to face the complexity of such issues as educational leadership, and to develop emotions to help them think with their hearts.[30] Students deepen their outer academic, conceptual, and social understandings through consistent attention to their reflective clarity, self-awareness, sense of purpose, and socio-emotional competencies. Students need to give full awareness, attention, and acceptance to the experience in front of them to access the presence that's there, beginning with interaction with their inner selves.

PRESENCE IN HUMAN-ENVIRONMENT INTERACTION

Environmental factors and personal habits of distraction may undermine online learners' focus and awareness. Here, it is important to bring a balanced attention to both digital and physical spaces. As noted earlier, students need a safe virtual environment to mitigate the ever-increasing challenge of digital disarray, especially since the computer screen acts as a gateway to learners' many concurrent responsibilities and interests.

To help students avoid the messiness of the digital world and instead experience the benefits of its multimodal access to their peers and instructors, I ask them to maintain a multistep digital decluttering practice throughout the course. This practice might involve emptying their email inboxes, organizing folders, suspending unnecessary digital subscriptions, consolidating bookmarks, cleansing social feeds, organizing passwords and log-ins. I send students periodic encouragement to declutter their virtual work corner so that it may serve as a reflective space:

> Good day! How are you? What is the quality of your attention now? Are you focused or distracted? Is your breathing fast, slow? Are you holding your breath? What is going on in your body? Are you relaxed, or do you notice any places of tension in your body? Please paste this message into a Word document (or equivalent) and follow the next prompts from there.
>
> Can you now take a few minutes to close all the windows you are not working on (keeping this window active)? Bookmark the tabs in your browser for future retrieval and close those you do not need; save the open files you are not currently working on and close them; turn your phone to the Do Not Disturb mode; turn on the Do Not Disturb mode on your computer; return to this window.
>
> Can you now take time to think about how you are attending to what is happening in the current moment? What is the quality of your attention now? Are you feeling any different . . . focused or distracted? Has your breathing changed? How are you feeling in your body? Are you relaxed or tensed? Are you feeling any different than you did before taking these digital decluttering steps? You can jot down what you are experiencing below.

Similarly, during our synchronous sessions, I begin by inviting students to close all the windows they are not using and to be present in the platform through which we are connecting, e.g., Teams or Zoom.

I often remind my students that contemplative and physical offline activities, such as a walk in the park, contribute to their online presence as they promote the mind-body-spirit connection and balance. As the pendulum of the physical-virtual presence of the online learner is constantly shifting between the outer and the inner world of the self, it is helpful to seek grounding in physical reality offline. By interacting with the physical world around them, especially the natural world, learners can "come home" to the here and now.

PRESENCE IN HUMAN-TECHNOLOGY INTERACTION

The learner's interaction with technology can either facilitate or constrain other forms of interaction. However, mere technological competency does not guarantee meaningful interaction and knowledge building in online learning environments.[31] Online students report that using too many tools and functions in a purposeless way adds to their confusion and overwhelm in the digital space.[32] Employing the right technologies for the right job in a meaningful way leads to higher levels of engagement with peers, instructors, and content, which, in turn, offers a more satisfying online learning experience. Incorporating technology in a way that minimizes its detriments and maximizes its benefits requires adequate levels of familiarity, awareness, and online-learning self-efficacy.[33] Supported by their confidence in the use of technology, learners can attend to the task at hand and be fully present in the process of technology-mediated connection and communication.

Still, with the glass screen separating us, with no physiological supports of being together and no embodied co-being in physical proximity, it might be energetically more challenging to enter into the virtual state of "collective effervescence"[34] of a shared virtual reality. It might require more intentional attention in the design of the online course and purposeful effort of participants to transcend the confines of technology (which are often emotional) and enjoy the state of "mixing of minds"[35] that fosters holistic copresence and defies the physical distance between students.

To avoid the experience of disembodied communication, disconnection, and interrupted mind-body-spirit presence, I introduce video-moderated body-movement activities such as collaborative meaning-making games and basic chair-yoga stretches. These are both real-time activities that learners can join during our synchronous sessions and prerecorded videos that offer students the opportunity to attune to their physicality and experience the sense of connection to themselves. Digital tools can hence mediate whole-person connection at a time and place of one's choosing and moderate communication that is not limited by the fear of technology. When comfortable with these tools, learners can interact with them and through them seamlessly so that the human–technology interaction can promote higher levels of presence.

CONCLUSION

It is possible to cultivate presence in online learning through learners' dynamic interactions with self and others: peers and teachers, content, technology, and both digital and physical environments. For online learning to be meaningful, it should be a whole-person experience learners intentionally engage in with their mind, body, spirit, and heart. While it is simpler to guide students toward presence in synchronous sessions and even offline activities, here-and-now feelings and experiences can also be captured in asynchronous learning artifacts for delayed human-content interaction.

Devoid of physiological connection and unable to use all of the senses to learn,[36] the tendency in online learning might be to favor the traditional digital-learning approaches that privilege the mind-intellect over the body-spirit.[37] Nevertheless, my graduate students' experiences demonstrate that contemplative practices can foster deep and reflective learning within the digital space. Through systematic practice in cultivating presence and embracing that practice in technology-mediated connections with self and others, most of them gained indispensable skills for the challenges they will face as education leaders in the twenty-first century. With a mindset that values inner reflective awareness and the capacity to balance it with cognitive, emotional, and physical abilities, students are better prepared to attend to their individual and collective challenges. Having practiced compassion and kindness in the online classroom, students will be able to extend it to themselves and others so that they can flourish as digital citizens and educational leaders.

For online classroom instructors, the approach described herein requires careful design to incorporate contemplative practices for students. Instructors' own sense of presence is undoubtedly a pillar of their learners' engagement. The sine qua non of presence in online learning is attention to what is in front of the participants, whether it is conveyed in a learning artifact, communication piece, or the face of a teacher in the Zoom space. That attention arises from the awareness of what is accessible and from the choice to attend to it without judgment. When in a place of trust and within an encouraging, loving community of learners, each individual can interact with the learning event with acceptance and surrender, without hiding behind the computer screen. This sharing of a virtual and spiritual space that is safe and free of distractions promotes openness and humility, inviting new insights and understandings.

NOTES

1. Lev S. Vygotsky, *Thought and Language* (Cambridge, MA: MIT Press, 2012; original work published 1934).

2. Agnieszka Palalas, "Mindfulness for Human-Centred Digital Learning," *Argentinian Journal of Applied Linguistics*, no. 2 (2019): 110–25.

3. John M. Dirkx, "The Meaning and Role of Emotions in Adult Learning," *New Directions for Adult and Continuing Education* 2008, no. 120 (2008): 7–18; Oren Ergas, "Descartes in a 'Headstand': Introducing 'Body-Oriented Pedagogy,'" *Paideusis* 21, no. 1 (2013): 4–12; David J. Nguyen and Jay B. Larson, "Don't Forget About the Body: Exploring the Curricular Possibilities of Embodied Pedagogy," *Innovative Higher Education* 40, no. 4 (2015): 331–44.

4. Wayne Teasdale, *The Mystic Heart: Discovering a Universal Spirituality in the World's Religions* (Novato, CA: New World Library, 2001).

5. Parker J. Palmer, *The Courage to Teach: Exploring the Inner Landscape of a Teacher's Life* (San Francisco, CA: John Wiley & Sons, 2017), 4.

6. Rob Koegel, "The Heart of Holistic Education: A Reconstructed Dialogue Between Ron Miller and Rob Koegel," *Encounter: Education for Meaning and Social Justice* 16, no. 2 (2003): 11–18.

7. Ibid., 15.

8. Ibid.

9. Michael G. Moore, "Theory of Transactional Distance," in T*heoretical Principles of Distance Education*, ed. Desmond Keegan (New York: Routledge, 1993), 22–38; Michael G. Moore, "The Theory of Transactional Distance," in *Handbook of Distance Education* (New York: Routledge, 2013), 84–103.

10. Ellen Rose, *On Reflection: An Essay on Technology, Education, and the Status of Thought in the 21st Century* (Toronto: Canadian Scholars' Press, 2013).

11. David M. Levy, *Mindful Tech: How to Bring Balance to Our Digital Lives* (New Haven: Yale University Press, 2016); Agnieszka Palalas, "Mindfulness in Mobile and Ubiquitous Learning: Harnessing the Power of Attention," in *Mobile and Ubiquitous Learning* (Singapore: Springer, 2018), 19–44.

12. Jon Kabat-Zinn, *Full Catastrophe Living: How to Cope with Stress, Pain and Illness Using Mindfulness Meditation*, rev. ed. (London: Hachette UK, 2013), 28–29.

13. Ellen J. Langer, "A Mindful Education," *Educational Psychologist* 28, no. 1 (1993): 43–50.

14. Ergas Oren and Sharon Todd, eds., *Philosophy East/West: Exploring Intersections Between Educational and Contemplative Practices* (West Sussex, UK: John Wiley & Sons, 2016).

15. Mark Pegrum and Agnieszka Palalas, "Attentional Literacy as a New Literacy: Helping Students Deal with Digital Disarray," *Canadian Journal of Learning and Technology* 47, no. 2 (2021), 8.

16. See, for example, D. Randy Garrison and Doug Shale, eds., *Education at a Distance: From Issues to Practice* (Malabar, FL: R. E. Krieger Publishing Company, 1990); Arthur W. Chickering and Zelda F. Gamson, "Seven Principles for Good Practice in Undergraduate Education," *AAHE Bulletin* 3 (1987): 7.

17. Nada Dabbagh, "The Online Learner: Characteristics and Pedagogical Implications," *Contemporary Issues in Technology and Teacher Education* 7, no. 3 (2007): 217–26; Debra Hoven, Rima Al Tawil, Kathryn Johnson, Nikki Pawlitschek, and Dan Wilton, "The Impact of a Cohort Model for Online Doctoral Student Retention and Success," *In Early Warning Systems and Targeted Interventions for Student Success in Online Courses* (IGI Global, 2020), 113–39.

18. Joseph B. Walther, "Selective Self-Presentation in Computer-Mediated Communication: Hyperpersonal Dimensions of Technology, Language, and Cognition," *Computers in Human Behavior* 23, no. 5 (2007): 2538–57.

19. Ram Dass and Mirabai Bush, *Walking Each Other Home: Conversations on Loving and Dying* (Louisville, CO: Sounds True, 2018).

20. Terry Anderson, "Teaching in an Online Learning Context," *Theory and Practice of Online Learning* 273 (Athabasca: Athabasca University Press, 2004); Florence Martin and Doris U. Bolliger, "Engagement Matters: Student Perceptions on the Importance of Engagement Strategies in the Online Learning Environment," *Online Learning* 22, no. 1 (2018): 205–22; Peter Shea, Chun S. Li, Karen Swan, and Alexandra Pickett, "Developing Learning Community in Online Asynchronous Col-

lege Courses: The Role of Teaching Presence," *Journal of Asynchronous Learning Networks* 9, no. 4 (2005): 59–82.

21. Michael F. Beaudoin, "Learning or Lurking?: Tracking the 'Invisible' Online Student." *The Internet and Higher Education* 5, no. 2 (2002): 147–55; Michael G. Moore, "Three Types of Interaction," *American Journal of Distance Education* 3, no. 2 (1989): 1–7.

22. Charalambos Vrasidas, "Constructivism versus Objectivism: Implications for Interaction, Course Design, and Evaluation in Distance Education," *International Journal of Educational Telecommunications* 6, no. 4 (2000): 339–62, 2.

23. Aubteen Darabi, Meagan C. Arrastia, David W. Nelson, Tom Cornille, and Xinya Liang, "Cognitive Presence in Asynchronous Online Learning: A Comparison of Four Discussion Strategies," *Journal of Computer Assisted Learning* 27, no. 3 (2011): 216–27.

24. Rose, *On Reflection*.

25. Ibid.

26. Keng-Soon Soo and Curt J. Bonk, "Interaction: What Does It Mean in Online Distance Education?" (1998). Paper presented at the Ed-Media and EdTelecom 98 Conference, Freibourg, Germany, 3.

27. Atsusi Hirumi, "A Framework for Analyzing, Designing, and Sequencing Planned Elearning Interactions," in *The Perfect Online Course: Best Practices for Designing and Teaching,* ed. Anymir Orellana, Terry L. Hudgins, and Michael Simonson (Charlotte, NC: Information Age Publishing, 2009), 201–28.

28. Poems by David Whyte can be accessed through his website: http://www.davidwhyte.com/.

29. Two examples of such practice can be found at these links: https://ggie.berkeley.edu/practice/mindful-breathing-for-adults/; https://ggie.berkeley.edu/practice/brief-body-scan/.

30. Arthur Zajonc, "Love and Knowledge: Recovering the Heart of Learning Through Contemplation." *Teachers College Record* 108, no. 9 (2006): 1742–59.

31. Sari Lindblom-Ylänne and Heikki Pihlajamäki, "Can a Collaborative Network Environment Enhance Essay-Writing Processes?" *British Journal of Educational Technology* 34, no. 1 (2003): 17–30.

32. Agnieszka Palalas, "Mindfulness in Mobile and Ubiquitous Learning: Harnessing the Power of Attention"; "Mindfulness for Human-Centred Digital Learning"; Agnieszka Palalas, Anastasia Mavraki, Kokkoni Drampala, Anna Krassa, and Christina Karakanta, "Mindfulness Practices in Online Learning: Supporting Learner Self-Regulation," *The Journal of Contemplative Inquiry* 7, no. 1 (2020).

33. Jihong Zhou and Hongying Yu, "Contribution of Social Support to Home-Quarantined Chinese College Students' Well-Being During The COVID-19 Pandemic: The Mediating Role of Online Learning Self-Efficacy and Moderating Role of Anxiety," *Social Psychology of Education* 24, no. 6 (2021): 1643–62.

34. Émile Durkheim, *The Elementary Forms of the Religious Life* (1912, English translation by Joseph Swain: 1915); translation by Karen E. Fields (New York: Free Press, 1995).

35. Pilar Jennings, *Mixing Minds: The Power of Relationship in Psychoanalysis and Buddhism* (Somerville, MA: Wisdom Publications, 2010).

36. John M. Dirkx, "The Meaning and Role of Emotions in Adult Learning"; Oren Ergas, "Descartes in a 'Headstand': Introducing 'Body-Oriented Pedagogy.'"

37. Roxana Ng, "Embodied Pedagogy as Transformative Learning: A Critical Reflection," in Canadian Association for the Study of Adult Education (CASAE) 2005 Conference Proceedings, 2005.

BIBLIOGRAPHY

Anderson, Terry. "Teaching in an Online Learning Context." *Theory and Practice of Online Learning*. Athabasca: Athabasca University Press, 2004.

Beaudoin, Michael F. "Learning or Lurking?: Tracking the 'Invisible' Online Student." *The Internet and Higher Education* 5, no. 2 (2002): 147–55.

Chickering, Arthur W., and Zelda F. Gamson. "Seven Principles for Good Practice in Undergraduate Education." *AAHE Bulletin* 3 (1987): 7.

Dabbagh, Nada. "The Online Learner: Characteristics and Pedagogical Implications." *Contemporary Issues in Technology and Teacher Education* 7, no. 3 (2007): 217–26.

Darabi, Aubteen, Meagan C. Arrastia, David W. Nelson, Tom Cornille, and Xinya Liang. "Cognitive Presence in Asynchronous Online Learning: A Comparison of Four Discussion Strategies." *Journal of Computer Assisted Learning* 27, no. 3 (2011): 216–27.

Dass, Ram, and Mirabai Bush. *Walking Each Other Home: Conversations on Loving and Dying*. Louisville, CO: Sounds True, 2018.

Dirkx, John M. "The Meaning and Role of Emotions in Adult Learning." *New Directions for Adult and Continuing Education*, no. 120 (2008): 7–18.

Durkheim, Émile. *The Elementary Forms of the Religious Life* (1912, English translation by Joseph Swain: 1915); translation by Karen E. Fields. New York: Free Press, 1995.

Ergas, Oren. "Descartes in a 'Headstand': Introducing 'Body-Oriented Pedagogy.'" *Paideusis* 21, no. 1 (2013): 4–12.

Ergas, Oren, and Sharon Todd, eds. *Philosophy East/West: Exploring Intersections Between Educational and Contemplative Practices*. West Sussex, UK: John Wiley & Sons, 2016.

Garrison, D. Randy, and Doug Shale, eds. *Education at a Distance: From Issues to Practice*. Malabar, FL: R. E. Krieger Publishing Company, 1990.

Hirumi, Atsusi. "A Framework for Analyzing, Designing, and Sequencing Planned Elearning Interactions," in *The Perfect Online Course: Best Practices for Designing and Teaching*, edited by Anymir Orellana, Terry L. Hudgins, and Michael Simonson, 201–28. Charlotte, NC: Information Age Publishing, 2009.

Hoven, Debra, Rima Al Tawil, Kathryn Johnson, Nikki Pawlitschek, and Dan Wilton. "The Impact of a Cohort Model for Online Doctoral Student Retention and Success." In *Early Warning Systems and Targeted Interventions for Student Success in Online Courses*, 113–39. Hershey, PA: IGI Global, 2020.

Jennings, Pilar. *Mixing Minds: The Power of Relationship in Psychoanalysis and Buddhism*. Somerville, MA: Wisdom Publications, 2010.

Kabat-Zinn, Jon. *Full Catastrophe Living: How to Cope with Stress, Pain and Illness Using Mindfulness Meditation*, rev. ed. London: Hachette UK, 2013.

Koegel, Rob. "The Heart of Holistic Education: A Reconstructed Dialogue Between Ron Miller and Rob Koegel." *Encounter: Education for Meaning and Social Justice* 16, no. 2 (2003): 11–18.

Langer, Ellen J. "A Mindful Education." *Educational Psychologist* 28, no. 1 (1993): 43–50.

———. "Mindful Learning." *Current Directions in Psychological Science* 9, no. 6 (2000): 220–23.

Levy, David M. *Mindful Tech: How to Bring Balance to Our Digital Lives*. New Haven: Yale University Press, 2016.

Lindblom-Ylänne, Sari, and Heikki Pihlajamäki. "Can a Collaborative Network Environment Enhance Essay-Writing Processes?" *British Journal of Educational Technology* 34, no. 1 (2003): 17–30.

Martin, Florence, and Doris U. Bolliger. "Engagement Matters: Student Perceptions on the Importance of Engagement Strategies in the Online Learning Environment." *Online Learning* 22, no. 1 (2018): 205–22.

Moore, Michael G. "Three Types of Interaction." *American Journal of Distance Education* 3, no. 2 (1989): 1–7.

———. "Theory of Transactional Distance," In *Theoretical Principles of Distance Education*, edited by Desmond Keegan, 22–38. New York: Routledge, 1993.

———. "The Theory of Transactional Distance." In *Handbook of Distance Education*, edited by Michael Moore, 84–103. New York: Routledge, 2013.

Ng, Roxana. "Embodied Pedagogy as Transformative Learning: A Critical Reflection." In Canadian Association for the Study of Adult Education (CASAE) 2005 Conference Proceedings. 2005.

Nguyen, David J., and Jay B. Larson. "Don't Forget About the Body: Exploring the Curricular Possibilities of Embodied Pedagogy." *Innovative Higher Education* 40, no. 4 (2015): 331–44.

Palalas, Agnieszka. "Mindfulness in Mobile and Ubiquitous Learning: Harnessing the Power of Attention." In *Mobile and Ubiquitous Learning*, edited by Shengquan Yu, Mohamed Ally, and Avgoustos Tsinakos, 19–44. Singapore: Springer, 2018.

———. "Mindfulness for Human-Centred Digital Learning." *Argentinian Journal of Applied Linguistics*, no. 2 (2019): 110–25.

Palalas, Agnieszka, Anastasia Mavraki, Kokkoni Drampala, Anna Krassa, and Christina Karakanta. "Mindfulness Practices in Online Learning: Supporting Learner Self-Regulation." *The Journal of Contemplative Inquiry* 7, no. 1 (2020).

Palmer, Parker J. *The Courage to Teach: Exploring the Inner Landscape of a Teacher's Life*. San Francisco, CA: John Wiley & Sons, 2017.

Pegrum, Mark, and Agnieszka Palalas. "Attentional Literacy as a New Literacy: Helping Students Deal with Digital Disarray." *Canadian Journal of Learning and Technology* 47, no. 2 (2021).

Rose, Ellen. *On Reflection: An Essay on Technology, Education, and the Status of Thought in the 21st Century.* Toronto: Canadian Scholars' Press, 2013.

Shea, Peter, Chun S. Li, Karen Swan, and Alexandra Pickett. "Developing Learning Community in Online Asynchronous College Courses: The Role of Teaching Presence." *Journal of Asynchronous Learning Networks* 9, no. 4 (2005): 59–82.

Soo, Keng-Soon, and Curt J. Bonk. "Interaction: What Does It Mean in Online Distance Education?." (1998). Paper presented at the Ed-Media and EdTelecom '98 conference, Freibourg, Germany.

Teasdale, Wayne. *The Mystic Heart: Discovering a Universal Spirituality in the World's Religions.* Novato, CA: New World Library, 2001.

Vrasidas, Charalambos. "Constructivism Versus Objectivism: Implications for Interaction, Course Design, and Evaluation in Distance Education." *International Journal of Educational Telecommunications* 6, no. 4 (2000): 339–62.

Vygotsky, Lev S. *Thought and Language.* Cambridge, MA: MIT Press, 2012.

Walther, Joseph B. "Selective Self-Presentation in Computer-Mediated Communication: Hyperpersonal Dimensions of Technology, Language, and Cognition." *Computers in Human Behavior* 23, no. 5 (2007): 2538–57. DOI: 10.1016/j.chb.2006.05.002

Zajonc, Arthur. "Love and Knowledge: Recovering the Heart of Learning through Contemplation." *Teachers College Record* 108, no. 9 (2006): 1742–59.

Zhou, Jihong, and Hongying Yu. "Contribution of Social Support to Home-Quarantined Chinese College Students' Well-Being during the COVID-19 Pandemic: The Mediating Role of Online Learning Self-Efficacy and Moderating Role of Anxiety." *Social Psychology of Education* 24, no. 6 (2021): 1643–62.

PAUSE

Get Up and Stretch

Chapter Three

Cultivating Emotional Presence

Building and Nurturing an Online Community of Inquiry

Deborah Dell

I recall my first experience in distance learning in an online Community of Inquiry like it was yesterday, although admittedly, at the time I had no idea of the vernacular or what exactly an online-learning Community of Inquiry was. I had embarked on taking a fully online master's program. From the very beginning, the learning format was completely foreign to me. The class was set up in such a way that the "teacher" seemed to be muted and only appeared to make comments that linked the learners to each other to deepen the unfolding discussion, never providing definitive answers.

Discussion-based teaching through online threaded discussion boards and reflective journals that asked us to link our own lifeworld with class content were two primary learning vehicles of that online learning class that were never part of my undergraduate education. In fact, I completed my entire undergraduate degree without ever talking to another learner about class content. The pedagogical contrast between this new master's program and my undergraduate face-to-face learning was stark. In my undergraduate in-person classrooms, the professors were largely positioned as experts who transmitted knowledge in long soliloquies. There were a few opportunities for student questions, but that space was largely taken up at the end of the class time, and by those in the front of the very large classroom.

It is true that strong emotions help to encode memories, and perhaps this lends support to why I remember my first online learning classes in such vivid detail. What I remember most about that first week of online learning was ultimately what compelled me to become a lifelong learner and eventually a strong advocate for the contemplative, mindful, purposeful enactment of emotional presence and Community of Inquiry distance-learning pedagogy.

Almost immediately after the start of my first online class, other students were angry. They were expressing the kind of anger that is born from confusion and fear of the unknown. The kind of anger that is made more comfortable if targeted outward rather than considered inward. The kind of anger that makes a person want to ruminate on and collect evidence for its justifications. The kind of anger that compels one to recruit others who may feel the same, so that the anger can be further fueled by collective justification, remain steadfast in the label of *anger* and never transform or fade to reveal the inner reality, the fear and vulnerability underneath.

My classmates behind the scenes were demanding to be "taught" by the instructor, rather than learn through the collective reflections and discussions that formed the bulk of the pedagogical tools. "What am I paying for?," "How can I know the 'right' answer if there are so many opinions?," and "I didn't come here to teach myself or learn from other students" were common refrains. Their reactions, of course, were twofold: For many, it was their first experience with online learning, and the professors had chosen not to use a standard lecture format, but to instead embrace elements of community-based learning woven together with specific pedagogical tools from a reflective and discussion-based pedagogy. When I look back on those first few weeks as an online learner, I am acutely aware of the disruptive potential of unidentified, untamed feelings, as well as their powerful influence as emotional contagions.

Ultimately, it was this memory that anchored my passion and compelled me to further study the importance of purposefully teaching about Community of Inquiry philosophical foundations before attempting to build or nurture an online Community of Inquiry (CoI). Armed with both a very personal and educationally informed perspective about CoI, I developed a passion for pedagogical tools that help learners to make the transformative shift from the individualistic, passive, and transmission-based learning models they have very often been largely socialized within.

It is from this springboard that this chapter seeks to extend the CoI framework to include emotional presence as part of social, cognitive, and teaching presence. I will also show the synergies between mindfulness-based pedagogy and CoI, and how mindfulness practices can enhance the emanation of a collective emotional presence.

In this chapter, I will first introduce the CoI framework, showing the parallels between mindfulness-based pedagogy and the CoI framework in online education. I argue that mindfulness practices can help to set a learning climate in which learners who are new to the CoI pedagogy in online education can sit with and work through their emotions and reactions to an unfamiliar learning model, and to move from being a passive learner to an active learner and co-teacher.

THE COMMUNITY OF INQUIRY FRAMEWORK

The CoI framework is a collaborative, constructivist-informed, distance-education pedagogical framework that highlights the importance of collaborative involvement in a learning community. As highlighted by Palalas in this edited volume, learner-to-learner interaction is a key component in the knowledge-creation process. CoI was developed by Garrison, Anderson, and Archer over a period of several years. The CoI framework was influenced and informed by a large body of work in philosophy, psychology, and educational research, including Vygotsky's, Dewey's, and Lipman's social constructivist ideas, that emphasize discussion-based teaching and shared knowledge construction.[1]

The CoI articulates three unique overlapping types of human presence—social, cognitive, and teaching—that converge to effect deep, meaningful learning through the creation and maintenance of an online learning community. The framework itself is a simplified heuristic for a complex theoretical belief system that captures ten subdimensions of the learning experience. Embedded in the overlaps between the three presences are three additional considerations that help propel the establishment of community cohesion and inquiry-based learning. These include a shared learner/teacher responsibility to regulate learning and contribute to a trusting and supportive climate that will support critically reflective discourse.

In 2000, when the researchers from the University of Calgary were developing the Community of Inquiry framework for online learning, they were certainly not concerned with connecting it to a parallel movement in largely place-based schools called mindfulness-based pedagogy. With the advantage of hindsight, I have come to believe, through examining the foundations of both movements, that CoI and mindfulness-based contemplative pedagogy share many parallels, including the strong emphasis away from didactic teaching methods in favor of collaboration and shared teaching space. It is similarly believed that "the nature of mindfulness seems to lend itself to nondidactic experiential learning/teaching strategies which allow students to explore practices at their own pace within a critical community of inquiry."[2]

In the Community of Inquiry framework, the definition of social presence has evolved through the benefit of much research into the construct and its component parts to be defined as "the ability of participants to identify with a group, communicate openly in a trusting environment, and develop personal and affective relationships progressively by way of projecting their individual personalities."[3] Cognitive presence "is defined as the extent to which learners are able to construct and confirm meaning through sustained reflection and discourse in a critical community of inquiry."[4] Lastly, teaching presence is concerned with design and facilitation as "a means to an end to support and enhance social and cognitive presence for the purpose of realizing educational outcomes."[5]

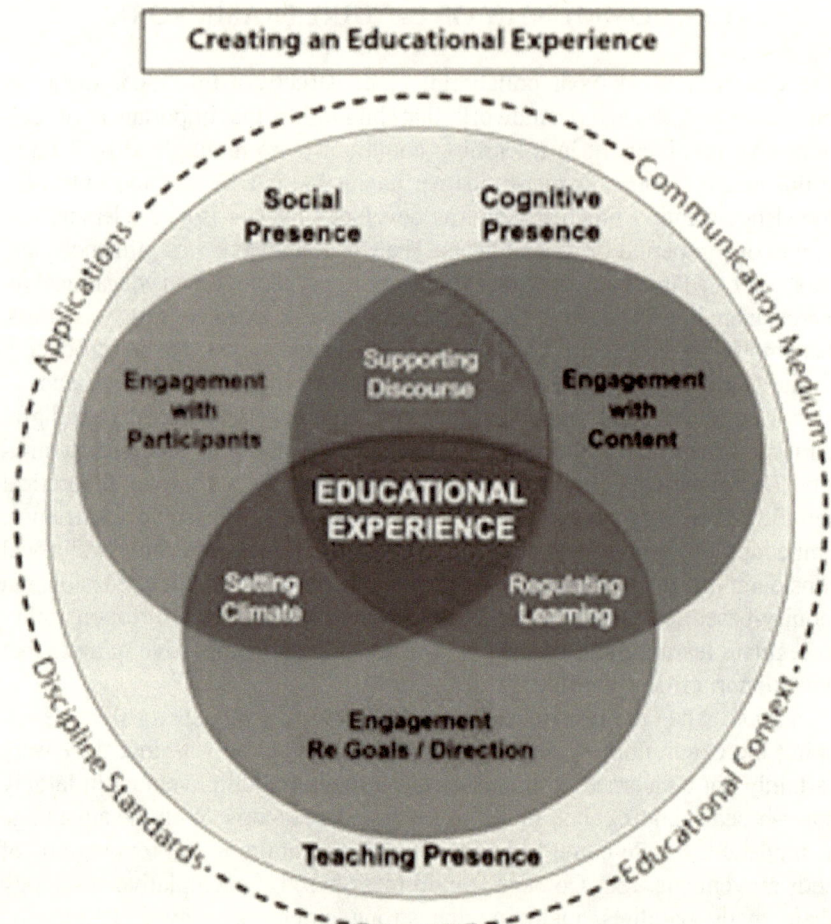

Figure 3.1. Community of Inquiry Framework. *Source*: creative commons license https://www.thecommunityofinquiry.org

In recent years CoI researchers have made attempts to reflect the understanding of emotions and their presence more broadly in both the regulating learning overlap that borders cognitive and teaching presence, and at the edges of all three presences.[6] Collectively these works speak to an increased need to be more mindful about the initial establishment of a CoI and the development of trust, belonging, and other socially situated emotions and affective states as foundational community-building precursors.

PARALLEL LINES, PARALLEL LENSES

Despite what was going on in that first online class that I described at the beginning of the chapter, I was able to keep a curious onlooker's perspective on the emotional turmoil and the burgeoning complaint culture. I wasn't having the same emotional reaction to the pedagogy as my peers. In reality, as a learner and an educator, I found it easy to accept and embrace the possibilities of CoI pedagogy since it seemed so ontologically and epistemologically congruent and natural to me.

I had spent the bulk of my career working and teaching in Indigenous mental health programs. These were programs that embraced contemplative ways of being and Indigenous healing methods that were naturally centered on shared space, and holistic, intersubjective learning mechanisms. With the advantage of hindsight, I can now see how closely the CoI's ideals aligned with my own workplace culture, workplace training, and epistemological stance. I was very comfortable with shared space, collective voice, honoring the multiplicity of ways of knowing, and contemplative and reflective ways of being as a means to learning and growth.

When I look back and try to articulate the ways in which the reflective contemplative practice I was accustomed to mirrors the CoI shared space, it's easy to see the parallel lines and parallel lenses in terms of foundational

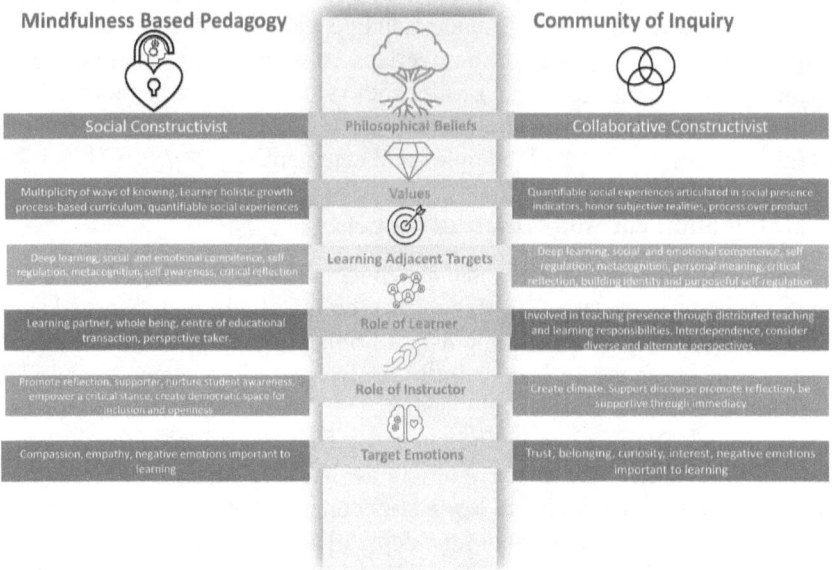

Figure 3.2. Mindfulness and Community of Inquiry Parallels. *Source*: Original for this chapter by Deborah Dell

philosophy, assumptions and values, and the intended learning and learning-adjacent outcomes. Secondarily, parallels exist in the way mindfulness-based pedagogy and CoI explicate role clarity for the learner and the educator. Lastly, both see the importance of the role of social and cognitive emotions and their importance in the learning journey.

Origins and Philosophical Foundations

The CoI developers recognize the thinking of foundational scholars like Dewey and Lipman. Embedded in the early beliefs about CoI is Dewey's conception of pedagogical practice as mediation rather than domination.[7] The strong connections to collaborative constructivist ways of knowing are woven throughout all the writings of Matthew Lipman.[8] Socio-cognitive or social constructivist labels are similarly given to mindfulness-based contemplative pedagogy.[9]

In both cases, the addition of the social or collaborative learning mechanisms strengthens the idea that contemplative or mindfulness-based ways of teaching reject a singular subjective reality and lead to a complex set of values and assumptions.

Values and Assumptions

The parallel between assumptions and principles is clear. Both CoI and mindfulness-based pedagogy anchor the importance of honoring the multiplicity of ways of knowing.[10] Both are concerned with learner holistic growth[11] and cultivating knowledge through understanding gained within the social milieu.[12] Both models emphasize the overlaps between social, emotional, and cognitive learning mechanisms. Lastly, both value and privilege process over products in the learning environment.[13] Both movements explain that the learning environment is both complex and emergent.

Learning and Learning-Adjacent Targets

It makes sense that frameworks that are concerned with learning see learning gains as the primary target. In this regard, both CoI and mindfulness-based pedagogy reference deep learning as the primary goal.[14] Mindfulness-based pedagogy has a focus on learner introspection and self-awareness, and CoI similarly targets learners actively searching for personal meaning, identity, and purpose.[15] Both CoI and mindfulness-based pedagogy specifically mention self-regulation and metacognition as learning-adjacent targets. CoI theorizing digs a little deeper to explicate a collective construct called *shared metacognition*.[16] In writings about the depth of CoI philosophy, shared metacognition is metaphorically an infinity loop between self- and co-regulation activities occurring in cycles as the learning endeavor transpires.[17]

Role of the Learner

Both mindfulness-based pedagogy and CoI imagine the role of the learner as the center of the learning environment and as an active partner in the learning transaction. As shown in Cleveland-Innes's chapter in this volume, CoI concretely explicates the learner's responsibility to be deeply involved in *teaching presence* through distributed teaching and learning responsibilities and learner reciprocity and interdependence.[18] What CoI describes as a responsibility to consider alternate and diverse perspectives, mindfulness-based pedagogy labels the responsibility for multiplicity in perspective taking.[19] Key in both is the belief that learning gets deeper and deeper through cycles of discussion, contemplation, and reflection.

Target Emotions

The importance of affective learning is considered in many learning frameworks, including both CoI and mindfulness-based contemplative pedagogy. In line with the spirit of mindfulness, Amann defines affective learning as "the acquisition of knowledge as a result of paying attention to and honouring our feelings and emotions."[20] Likewise, emotions have been identified as one of the key instructional goals of CoI since the framework's inception. In CoI, labeled emotions and affective states are framed as precursors to CoI creation. The emotional/affective labels of *trust* and *belonging* are primary targets for the establishment of a learning community. The labeled affective state of curiosity has been articulated as connected to deep learning in the inquiry process.[21] Likewise, in many definitions of mindfulness, maintaining a curious stance is a primary attitude.

Across all three CoI presences, the design elements incorporated in CoI and its two key research tools are filled with both affectively labeled anchors and emotional conjectures. Emotions and their importance in online learning are primarily included as the gravity of Community of Inquiry and a centrifugal force as outlined by the philosophical foundations of both mindfulness-based pedagogy and CoI.[22]

Heuristically, in the original CoI model, emotional presence was primarily explained in terms of emotional expression as a subcomponent of social presence. Much work has gone into CoI since that time, and the understanding of emotional presence has come to be known in a deeper, more connected way as intimately linked with the articulation and enactment of all three, social, teaching, and cognitive presence.

My own research work together with the work of Cleveland-Innes and Campbell highlights the complexity of the connection. According to a research study that captured the collective voices of experienced CoI learners and facilitators, graphically portraying and explicating a unique emotional presence is not logically or theoretically warranted, and may not adequately represent the interconnectedness of the model's component parts. However, there is utility in reformulating the definition of emotional presence to include the recognition that emotional presence may be a diffuse presence. Suggesting emotional presence as embodied through each of the three other presences, ultimately defining affective or emotional presence as "an intentional, deliberative discourse-based climate setting and self and coregulation (macro cognitive) manifested through the intersections of teaching, cognitive and social presence."[23] Key in this suggested reformulation was the mindful recognition that all three presences are relational and emotionally or affectively anchored. Social in belongingness, teaching in sharing gifts and insights, and cognitive in the collaborative constructivist and multiplicity of ways of knowing that inform the critical reflection goals. At the edges of the three articulated CoI presences lives space for an emotional presence that specific facilitation behaviors can massage to promote all of the aforementioned learning and learning-adjacent outcomes.

My own doctoral study confirmed the importance of emotional presence, emotional literacy, emotional attuning, and emotional regulation and navigation as important aspects of CoI learning. These same emotional targets are consistent in mindfulness-based contemplative pedagogies, as are the understanding of emotions as drivers of learning in technology-supported environments.[24]

Role of the Instructor

Jumping off from the importance of emotions and from the shared belief that the learner is actively involved in the learning environment, it stands to reason that both mindfulness-based pedagogy and CoI envision the instructor's role as more muted and facilitation-focused. That is not to say the responsibility is in any way lessened by the complexity of facilitation requirements, as both CoI and mindfulness-based pedagogy see presence as essential in creating the climate and holding space for the emergence of safe and shared construction of knowledge. In a study using CoI as a faculty development and assessment framework, many respondents felt teaching online required them to be more attentive to the needs of students.[25] Those attentive responsibilities are replete in the writings about both mindfulness-based pedagogy and CoI in the explanation of the facilitator as a supporter, nurturer, and promoter.

Key facilitation roles include supporting learner autonomy, discourse, and reflection, as well as empowering learners in both content exploration and taking critically reflective stances.[26] The instructor's role in CoI is one that requires facilitative acts that create the environmental conditions that allow shared knowledge construction to flourish, including recognizing and cultivating the multiplicity of paths to knowledge and modeling comfort with sitting with uncertainty and dissonance.[27]

MARRYING MINDFULNESS AND COMMUNITY OF INQUIRY: EMOTIONALLY PRESENT PEDAGOGY

The story at the start of this chapter, if analyzed by neuroscientists, would likely be categorized within the realm of the emotionally reactive fight, flight, or freeze response. Many of the students were faced with overwhelming emotions that are all too common when *rules of engagement* are abruptly changed. The unfamiliar CoI pedagogy that requires the learner to be active in contributing to the social, teaching, and cognitive presence in the classroom violates many of the rules we have lived with for the entirety of our formal education. The move from passive to active, from learner only to learner as co-teacher, and the shift of the teacher from sole expert to co-learner was jarring. No one really knew "how" to be a learner in this unfamiliar environment. While the story demonstrates only one emotional point in the eventual establishment of that particular Community of Inquiry, it paints a common picture of the strong emotions present in early class formation and educational adjustment situations.

My own education has been with one foot in counseling psychology and one foot in online instruction. Perhaps the strongest lesson I learned about how to facilitate and contribute to co-regulation in the face of the fight, flight, or freeze emotional response comes from the metaphor of emotions as chess pieces. In chess, each piece can only move according to established rules. The same is true of emotions. A person can't move from fear and vulnerability-fueled anger to active curiosity in the learning community, without first moving through other adjacent emotions, slowly reducing intensity and energy and moving through neutral reflective emotions toward curiosity, engagement, and openness. Likewise, in chess, moving one piece methodically and according to its rules creates space for other pieces to emerge from their confines. In psychological studies, rumination on negative emotions (having the chess piece stuck) has been shown to be mediated by the specific practice of mindfulness. The RAIN acronym[28]—recognition, acceptance, investigation, nurturance, developed by Michelle McDonald and modified and popularized by Tara Brach, and used in many mindfulness interventions—has parallel considerations.

PROPELLING A COMMUNITY OF INQUIRY: PLANTING THE ROOTS TO GROW THE FRUITS

In 2017 CoI researchers explicated their belief about the complexity of emotional tasks in CoI when they advised that emotions have "a pervasive influence on all aspects of a community of inquiry."[29] Therefore, a major consideration in CoI is the three-component reciprocal relationships and factors that enhance each other.[30] While managing the emotional pervasiveness, a facilitator in CoI has the responsibility for nurturing the establishment and gradual development of an inquiry-based trusting and safe learning community. This includes responsibility for very specific macrocognitive processes that simultaneously deal with the collective emotionally laden tasks of directing attention, sensemaking, planning, maintaining common ground, and building knowledge in collaborative contexts.[31]

Garrison outlines that the challenge for educators is to make sense of the complexity of the ideas presented in the CoI framework and apply them pragmatically to unique educational environments.[32] Making sense and becoming pragmatic can be achieved by considering all of the conjectures included in the CoI framework in a more practical order.

Figure 3.3 depicts an exploded model of the Community of Inquiry framework. Exploding the model to reveal its component parts helps us to explicate and contemplate the specific pedagogical tools contained in the centrifuge (propeller of the model) and the overlaps between the presences. This highlights the early-stage importance of the mutually reinforcing overlaps of the framework and illuminates the importance of three central facilitation tasks: setting the climate; supporting discourse; and regulating learning.

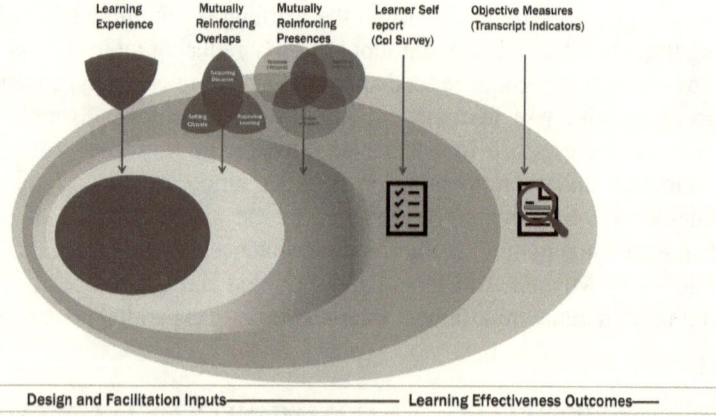

Figure 3.3. Exploded Model of Community of Inquiry Design Conjectures. *Source*: Dell, Deborah. "Emotional Presence in Community of Inquiry: A Scoping Review and Delphi Study." Athabasca University, 2021. http://hdl.handle.net/10791/361.

Mindfully Setting the Climate

In the COI framework, the overlap between teaching and social presence is called *setting the climate*. As with all other roles in CoI, it is a shared role between facilitator and learners. In a recent research study, learners and facilitators talked about pedagogical climate-setting behaviors that support emotional presence as: setting a tone; recognizing learners as whole beings; creating safe exploration space; role-modeling emotional vulnerability; and being explicit about the importance of learner–learner interaction as a foundational philosophy.[33] Leslie and Camargo-Borges outline climate setting and further explicate the importance of this role as managing and encouraging a multiplicity of ways of knowing through vulnerably exposing ourselves and practicing acceptance of others' worldviews.[34]

> **PRACTICAL APPLICATION: MINDFULLY SETTING CLIMATE**
>
>
>
> 1. Provide a warm welcome as learners check in. This can include silent or shared (through a debrief) contemplation on who they are as learners as they embark on this new learning journey.
> 2. Invite exploration of topics from multiple lenses. This can even mean assigning lenses to create dissonance. Create mindful attention and empathic response to others' worldviews by asking learners to imagine what it is like to be in the "shoes" of another learner before they craft a response in discussion boards.
> 3. Recognize that learners have lives replete with experiential learning that in some way might connect to the content. A gratitude exercise centered on taking the gifts from life learning can help to frame content connections.
> 4. Use feeling labels to increase emotional literacy and content connection. Model that it is acceptable to be angered, saddened, or elated by content. Teach nonjudgmental awareness and that there is wisdom to be gained from navigating through all feelings.
> 5. Link learners to each other in creative ways, and encourage jumping-off points for deeper discussion. Encourage mindful perspective-taking through question prompts and in progress dialogue.

6. Invite a multiplicity of ways of knowing as a means to privilege curiosity, community, and collaborative construction over completeness or competition. Use perspective-taking mindfulness activities to teach discussion forum etiquette, question prompts, and in-progress dialogue.

Mindfully Supporting Discourse

At the border of social and cognitive presence is supporting discourse. Supporting discourse in an emotionally present way points to the need to frame decisions about supporting the discussion-based teaching strategies through fostering and promoting emotional responses to content; offering individualized examples; exhibiting empathy in interactions; and developing supportive and affirming feedback. Deliberate, intentional, discussion-based strategies can aid in moving the collective toward deeper learning outcomes. Previous studies have confirmed that peer communication is significant in emotional transitions and, importantly, has been linked with emotional regulation, including reducing anxiety and increasing participation. This aspect of CoI mirrors mindfulness practices of attuned communication and response flexibility.

PRACTICAL APPLICATION: MINDFULLY SUPPORTING DISCOURSE

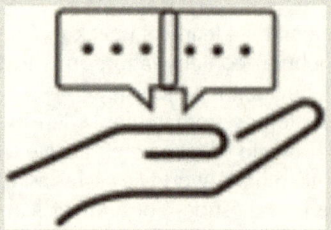

1. Use deliberative dialogue strategies that encourage a wide range of opinions and perspectives. Model attempts to see the world as others see it by employing attuned communication and actively listening to the roots of response, using *I hear, I see, I feel* sentence starters.
2. Support and encourage the use of emotion words in dialogue and emotional reactions to content by encouraging awareness and curiosity about the meaning connected to the emotion. Increase emotional literacy through present-focused and bodily awareness of emotional indicators.

3. Provide personalized examples to add real-world connection in content. This includes being open about your own emotional transitions of evolving connections to course content (i.e., using sentences that start with "I used to think . . .").
4. Use positive, affirming feedback strategies that help learners to focus on where there is strength in their reflections, and where they might find room for deeper reflection.
5. Encourage peer-to-peer dialogue as a means to reduce discomfort and encourage co-regulation. Reward instances of peers stretching their thinking by noting the learning level gains.
6. Be flexible in response strategies, continually promoting that there is not a binary right or wrong in deeper discussion questions.

Mindfully Regulating Learning

Straddling teaching and cognitive presence in the CoI framework is the overlap entitled regulating learning. As established previously in the chapter, regulating learning in the sense of a CoI is broader than self-regulation and includes aspects of co-regulation. That is to say, the regulating-learning overlap is both complex and multidirectional, including learner-to-learner and learner-to-teacher interactions. It involves emotionally congruent pedagogical tasks like igniting motivation by choosing discussion prompts; acknowledging that learning is emotional; seeing learners as whole beings; modeling emotional reactions to the content; and encouraging learners as teachers. In essence, it means calling on facilitators to honor emotions as learning drivers in three distinct ways: as an aid to cognition, as motivators, and as a means for creating collective responsibility.

Regulation is a complex construct that is both nested in and nested with other constructs. It involves both internal and external, subjective and objective cycles. Garrison describes regulation as simultaneously concerned with understanding knowledge inputs, monitoring, sustaining motivation, reflection in and on the action, and self- and co-regulating in the learning community.[35]

Similarly, many mindfulness practitioners draw on the popularized work of Jon Kabat-Zinn, which captures the essence of mindfulness as having three key parts: paying attention on purpose; staying present-focused; and embracing nonjudgmental awareness. As Pegrum and Palalas remind us, the articulation of "nonjudgment" does not mean that a learner is meant to operate void of any evaluative stance, but rather the nonjudgmental attitude is about creating space in the self and regulating in a way to become aware of reactivity and habitual judgments in favor of reflective response.[36]

This sentiment parallels the foundational philosophical idea in CoI that a critical Community of Inquiry is not one that avoids reasoned discussion or disagreement, but rather, nurtures and encourages the respectful challenging and testing of new ideas to realize collective knowledge.[37] In a technology-based CoI, the spaced learning opportunities (asynchronous) provide opportunities for both the development of mutually reflective communication and the contemplative goals and component parts of mindsight. Although Siegel[38] sees technology as a detractor to the cultivation of mindsight, CoI as a comprehensive online-learning framework provides a systematic articulation of presence and tools to be realized as enablers in this process. Like CoI, a mindful approach entails "the continuous creation of new categories; openness to new information; and an implicit awareness of more than one perspective."[39] These cycles of awareness can lead to a form of self- and co-regulation through sustained and attuned communication. This infinitely repeated cycle leads to both interpersonal and intrapersonal attunement, internal-external, subjective-objective cycles that form the core of the Community of Inquiry discussion-based teaching focus.

PRACTICAL APPLICATION: MINDFULLY REGULATING LEARNING

1. Choose question prompts that are emotionally resonant, and lend themselves to reflective attention.
2. Create space for reflection in and on action through assignments that require present-focused awareness connected to the topic.
3. Acknowledge emotional aspects of learning when they appear in discussion.
4. Model emotional recognition and emotional literacy in all learning interactions. Teach the RAIN strategy (recognition, acceptance, investigation, nurturance) as a regulative tool.
5. Encourage perspective-taking through promoting mindfulness interventions that focus on breathing awareness, and honest and sustained reflection before response.

CONCLUSION

The story at the beginning of the chapter is one that could be squarely placed in the realm of educational adjustment. Coaching for adjustment is crucial when learners are faced with the unfamiliar pedagogical tools that are often present in online and distance learning. In addition, recent events in the world have shed light on the need for education programs to be more closely attuned to a learner's entire lifeworld and holistic health functioning. The good news is that mindfulness-based contemplative pedagogy may not only aid in educational adjustment, and enhance emotional and mental health functioning, but additionally may serve as a protective factor against the development of mental health issues. This is partially because mindfulness-based interventions impact a broad range of emotional processes that are related to educational settings, including emotional regulation, mood states, stress coping, and burnout. By practicing more mindful emotional presence in relation to learning, facilitators can help model tools for emotional regulation and shared social regulation.

There is no doubt that as educators across the world grapple with returning to the "new normal," they need to pay attention to retaining all the benefits that the pivot to online learning has realized for many learners. Community of Inquiry when developed with attention to mindfulness-based practice has a promising future in terms of helping with educational adjustment, holistic education, and nurturing and embracing a respectful and collective spirit for collaboratively co-constructive ways of knowing.

NOTES

1. Randy Garrison, Terry Anderson, and Walter Archer, "Critical Inquiry in a Text-Based Environment: Computer Conferencing in Higher Education," *The Internet and Higher Education* 2, no. 2–3 (2000): 90, doi:10.1016/S1096-7516(00)00016-6.

2. Terry Hyland, "The Limits of Mindfulness: Emerging Issues for Education," *British Journal of Educational Studies* 64, no. 1 (January 2, 2016): 97–117, doi:10.1080/00071005.2015.1051946.

3. D. R. Garrison, *E-Learning in the 21st Century: A Framework for Research and Practice*, 2nd ed. (New York: Routledge, 2011), 23.

4. Randy Garrison, Terry Anderson, and Walter Archer, "Critical Thinking, Cognitive Presence, and Computer Conferencing in Distance Education," *American Journal of Distance Education* 15, no. 1 (January 1, 2001): 11, doi:10.1080/08923640109527071.

5. Ibid.

6. Martha Cleveland-Innes and Prisca Campbell, "Emotional Presence, Learning, and the Online Learning Environment," *International Review of Research in Open & Distance Learning* 13, no. 4 (December 2012): 269–92; Deborah Dell, "Emotional Presence in Community of Inquiry: A Scoping Review and Delphi Study" (Athabasca University, 2021), http://hdl.handle.net/10791/361; Deborah Dell and Norm Vaughan, "Fostering Student Self- and Co-Regulation in a Community of Inquiry," in *Community of Inquiry*, ed. Stefan Stenbom, Martha Cleveland-Innes, and Randy Garrison (New York: Routledge, in press); Susi Peacock and John Cowan, "From Presences to Linked Influences within Communities of Inquiry," *The International Review of Research in Open and Distributed Learning* 17, no. 5 (September 26, 2016), doi:10.19173/irrodl.v17i5.2602.

7. Randy Garrison and Terry Anderson, *E-Learning in the 21st Century: A Framework for Research and Practice* (New York: RoutledgeFalmer, 2003).

8. Randy Garrison, "Theoretical Foundations and Epistemological Insights of the Community of Inquiry," in *Educational Communities of Inquiry: Theoretical Framework, Research and Practice*, ed. Zehra Akyol and Randy Garrison (IGI Global, 2013), doi:10.4018/978-1-4666-2110-7.

9. Ellen J. Langer, "A Mindful Education," *Educational Psychologist* 28, no. 1 (1993): 43–50, doi:10.1207/s15326985ep2801_4.

10. Laura Roche Chapman, "Contemplative Pedagogy: Creating Mindful Educators and Classrooms," Tutorial, *ASHA Wire* (American Speech-Language-Hearing Association, 2021), world, doi:10.1044/2021_PERSP-21-00065; Randy Garrison, "Theoretical Foundations and Epistemological Insights of the Community of Inquiry," 2013.

11. Jennifer Ngan Bacquet, "Comparative Analysis of Contemplative Pedagogy and Its Possible Applications within Current International Education," *Thesis* 9, no. 2 (2020): 21.

12. Paula Gardner, "Contemplative Pedagogy: Fostering Transformative Learning in a Critical Service Learning Course," *Journal of Experiential Education* 44, no. 2 (June 2021): 152–66, doi:10.1177/1053825920952086; Garrison, "Theoretical Foundations and Epistemological Insights of the Community of Inquiry," 2013.

13. Garrison, "Theoretical Foundations and Epistemological Insights of the Community of Inquiry," 2013; Hyland, "The Limits of Mindfulness."

14. Bacquet, "Comparative Analysis of Contemplative Pedagogy and Its Possible Applications within Current International Education."

15. Randy Garrison, *E-Learning in the 21st Century: A Community of Inquiry Framework for Research and Practice* (New York: Routledge, Taylor & Francis Group, 2017).

16. Randy Garrison, "Shared Metacognition in a Community of Inquiry," *Online Learning* 26, no. 1 (March 1, 2022), doi:10.24059/olj.v26i1.3023.

17. Randy Garrison and Zehra Akyol, "Thinking Collaboratively in Educational Environments: Shared Metacognition and Co-Regulation in Communities of Inquiry," in *Educational Developments, Practices and Effectiveness*, ed. Jennifer Lock, Petrea Redmond, and Patrick Alan Danaher (London: Palgrave Macmillan UK, 2015), 39–52, doi:10.1057/9781137469939_3.

18. Garrison, *E-Learning in the 21st Century*.

19. Langer, "A Mindful Education."

20. Tara L Amann, "Creating Space for Somatic Ways of Knowing within Transformative Learning Theory," in C. A. Wiessner, S. R. Meyer, N. L. Pfhal, and P. G. Neaman (eds.), *Teacher's College* (Fifth International Conference on Transformative Learning, Columbia: Columbia University, 2003), 30.

21. Garrison, "Theoretical Foundations and Epistemological Insights of the Community of Inquiry," 2013.

22. Ibid.

23. Dell, "Emotional Presence in Community of Inquiry: A Scoping Review and Delphi Study," 90.

24. Kristina Loderer, Reinhard Pekrun, and James C. Lester, "Beyond Cold Technology: A Systematic Review and Meta-Analysis on Emotions in Technology-Based Learning Environments," *Learning and Instruction*, November 9, 2018, doi:10.1016/j.learninstruc.2018.08.002.

25. Mattyna L. Stephens and Joellen Coryell, "Faculty Perspectives on Context, Benefits, and Challenges in Fully Online Graduate Adult Education Programs," *Adult Learning* 32, no. 2 (May 2021): 79–88, doi:10.1177/1045159520959468.

26. Bacquet, "Comparative Analysis of Contemplative Pedagogy and Its Possible Applications within Current International Education."

27. Paul Leslie and Celiane Camargo-Borges, "Education as Community Affair: Digitally Designing Knowledge," *International Journal of E-Learning & Distance Education / Revue Internationale du e-Learning et la Formation* à *Distance* 37, no. 1 (May 11, 2022), doi:10.55667/ijede.2022.v37.i1.1219.

28. Tara Brach, "Recognize * Allow * Investigate * Nurture," *Spirituality & Health Magazine* (March 1, 2020).

29. Garrison, *E-Learning in the 21st Century: A Community of Inquiry Framework for Research and Practice*, 31.

30. Zehra Akyol, D. Randy Garrison, and M. Yasar Ozden, "Development of a Community of Inquiry in Online and Blended Learning Contexts," *Procedia—Social and Behavioral Sciences*, World Conference on Educational Sciences: New Trends and Issues in Educational Sciences, 1, no. 1 (January 1, 2009): 1834–38, doi:10.1016/j.sbspro.2009.01.324.

31. Stephen M. Fiore et al., "Towards an Understanding of Macrocognition in Teams: Developing and Defining Complex Collaborative Processes and Products," *Theoretical Issues in Ergonomics Science* 11, no. 4 (July 2010): 250–71, doi:10.1080/14639221003729128.

32. Garrison, *E-Learning in the 21st Century: A Community of Inquiry Framework for Research and Practice*.

33. Dell, "Emotional Presence in Community of Inquiry: A Scoping Review and Delphi Study."

34. Leslie and Camargo-Borges, "Education as Community Affair."

35. Garrison, "Theoretical Foundations and Epistemological Insights of the Community of Inquiry," 2013.

36. Mark Pegrum and Agnieszka Palalas, "Attentional Literacy as a New Literacy: Helping Students Deal with Digital Disarray / La Littératie Attentionnelle Comme Nouvelle Littératie: Aider Les Élèves à Faire Face Au Désarroi Numérique," *Canadian Journal of Learning & Technology* 47, no. 2 (Summer 2021): 1–18, doi:10.21432/cjlt28037.

37. Garrison, "Theoretical Foundations and Epistemological Insights of the Community of Inquiry," 2013.

38. D. Siegel, "Mindful Awareness, Mindsight, and Neural Integration," *Humanistic Psychologist* (United States: Taylor & Francis, January 1, 2009).

39. Ellen J. Langer, *The Power of Mindful Learning* (Massachusetts: Perseus Books, 2016), 4.

BIBLIOGRAPHY

Akyol, Zehra, D. Randy Garrison, and M. Yasar Ozden. "Development of a Community of Inquiry in Online and Blended Learning Contexts." Procedia—Social and Behavioral Sciences, World Conference on Educational Sciences: New Trends and Issues in Educational Sciences, 1, no. 1 (January 1, 2009): 1834–38. doi:10.1016/j.sbspro.2009.01.324.

Amann, Tara L. "Creating Space for Somatic Ways of Knowing Within Transformative Learning Theory." In C. A. Wiessner, S. R. Meyer, H. L. Pfhal, and P. G. Neaman, P.G. (eds), *Teacher's College*, 26–32. Columbia: Columbia University, 2003.

Bacquet, Jennifer Ngan. "Comparative Analysis of Contemplative Pedagogy and Its Possible Applications within Current International Education." *Thesis* 9, no. 2 (2020): 21.

Brach, Tara. "Recognize * Allow * Investigate * Nurture." *Spirituality & Health Magazine*, March 1, 2020.

Chapman, Laura Roche. "Contemplative Pedagogy: Creating Mindful Educators and Classrooms." Tutorial. ASHA Wire. American Speech-Language-Hearing Association, 2021. World. doi:10.1044/2021_PERSP-21-00065.

Cleveland-Innes, Martha, and Prisca Campbell. "Emotional Presence, Learning, and the Online Learning Environment." *International Review of Research in Open & Distance Learning* 13, no. 4 (December 2012): 269–92.

Dell, Deborah. "Emotional Presence in Community of Inquiry: A Scoping Review and Delphi Study." Athabasca University, 2021. http://hdl.handle.net/10791/361.

Dell, Deborah, and Norm Vaughan. "Fostering Student Self- and Co-Regulation in a Community of Inquiry." In *Community of Inquiry*, edited by Stefan Stenbom, Martha Cleveland-Innes, and Randy Garrison. New York: Routledge, in press.

Fiore, Stephen M., Kimberly A. Smith-Jentsch, Eduardo Salas, Norman Warner, and Michael Letsky. "Towards an Understanding of Macrocognition in Teams: Developing and Defining Complex Collaborative Processes and Products." *Theoretical Issues in Ergonomics Science* 11, no. 4 (July 2010): 250–71. doi:10.1080/14639221003729128.

Gardner, Paula. "Contemplative Pedagogy: Fostering Transformative Learning in a Critical Service Learning Course." *Journal of Experiential Education* 44, no. 2 (June 2021): 152–66. doi:10.1177/1053825920952086.

Garrison, D. Randy. *E-Learning in the 21st Century: A Framework for Research and Practice*, 2nd ed. New York: Routledge, 2011.

———. *E-Learning in the 21st Century: A Community of Inquiry Framework for Research and Practice*. New York: Routledge, 2017.

———. "Shared Metacognition in a Community of Inquiry." *Online Learning* 26, no. 1 (March 1, 2022). doi:10.24059/olj.v26i1.3023.

———. "Theoretical Foundations and Epistemological Insights of the Community of Inquiry." In *Educational Communities of Inquiry: Theoretical Framework, Research and Practice*, edited by Zehra Akyol and Randy Garrison. IGI Global, 2013. doi:10.4018/978-1-4666-2110-7.

Garrison, D. Randy, and Zehra Akyol. "Thinking Collaboratively in Educational Environments: Shared Metacognition and Co-Regulation in Communities of Inquiry." In *Educational Developments, Practices and Effectiveness*, edited by Jennifer Lock, Petrea Redmond, and Patrick Alan Danaher, 39–52. London: Palgrave Macmillan UK, 2015. doi:10.1057/9781137469939_3.

Garrison, Randy, and Terry Anderson. *E-Learning in the 21st Century: A Framework for Research and Practice*. New York: RoutledgeFalmer, 2003.

Garrison, Randy, Terry Anderson, and Walter Archer. "Critical Inquiry in a Text-Based Environment: Computer Conferencing in Higher Education." *The Internet and Higher Education* 2, no. 2–3 (2000): 87–105. doi:10.1016/S1096-7516(00)00016-6.

———. "Critical Thinking, Cognitive Presence, and Computer Conferencing in Distance Education." *American Journal of Distance Education* 15, no. 1 (January 1, 2001): 7–23. doi:10.1080/08923640109527071.

Hyland, Terry. "The Limits of Mindfulness: Emerging Issues for Education." *British Journal of Educational Studies* 64, no. 1 (January 2, 2016): 97–117. doi:10.1080/00071005.2015.1051946.

Langer, Ellen J. "A Mindful Education." *Educational Psychologist* 28, no. 1 (1993): 43–50. doi:10.1207/s15326985ep2801_4.

———. *The Power of Mindful Learning*. Cambridge, MA: Perseus Books, 2016.

Leslie, Paul, and Celiane Camargo-Borges. "Education as Community Affair: Digitally Designing Knowledge." *International Journal of E-Learning & Distance Education / Revue Internationale du e-Learning et la Formation à Distance* 37, no. 1 (May 11, 2022). doi:10.55667/ijede.2022.v37.i1.1219.

Loderer, Kristina, Reinhard Pekrun, and James C. Lester. "Beyond Cold Technology: A Systematic Review and Meta-Analysis on Emotions in Technology-Based Learning Environments." *Learning and Instruction*, November 9, 2018. doi:10.1016/j.learninstruc.2018.08.002.

Peacock, Susi, and John Cowan. "From Presences to Linked Influences within Communities of Inquiry." *The International Review of Research in Open and Distributed Learning* 17, no. 5 (September 26, 2016). doi:10.19173/irrodl.v17i5.2602.

Pegrum, Mark, and Agnieszka Palalas. "Attentional Literacy as a New Literacy: Helping Students Deal with Digital Disarray / La Littératie Attentionnelle Comme Nouvelle Littératie : Aider Les Élèves à Faire Face Au Désarroi Numérique." *Canadian Journal of Learning & Technology* 47, no. 2 (Summer 2021): 1–18. doi:10.21432/cjlt28037.

Siegel, D. "Mindful Awareness, Mindsight, and Neural Integration." *Humanistic Psychologist*. United States: Taylor & Francis, January 1, 2009.

Stephens, Mattyna L., and Joellen Coryell. "Faculty Perspectives on Context, Benefits, and Challenges in Fully Online Graduate Adult Education Programs." *Adult Learning* 32, no. 2 (May 2021): 79–88. doi:10.1177/1045159520959468.

Chapter Four

Vignette 1

Support for Contemplative Pedagogy through Shared Teaching Presence

Martha Cleveland-Innes

It is an honor to present my ever-evolving views about teaching as I journey between teacher presence and teaching presence. My journey is one shaped by changing societal characteristics as globalization and digitization creep into all that humans do. According to UNESCO, global education's response to these changes must be rooted in cooperation and collaboration among teachers and learners.[1] We can expect contemporary teaching and learning to bridge social, informational, and physical distances through *relationality* and *interaction*.

The concept of teach*er* presence emerged among those involved in teaching and learning development. Teacher presence refers to a process required to support cooperation and collaboration among students and teachers and between students. This activity is now a necessary part of education and the world our graduates will enter. Drawing on the definition from Thomas and Thorpe, *teacher presence* refers to a "complex mix of the teacher's persona and includes characteristics such as his or her openness, humanness, humility, authenticity, and engagement with the group."[2] This vignette will describe the evolution of my practices of teacher presence: in person, online, and a blend of both.

The first course I taught using technology by teleconference was in 1996—by accident. I had just graduated from my PhD program when my supervisor stopped me in the hallway. She asked me if I would be willing to teach research methods to the master of education students. I enthusiastically said yes, and asked several questions about dates and paperwork. As my supervisor stepped away from our brief but impactful engagement, she said, "By the way, this course is offered by teleconference. You must get in touch with the telephone bridge operator on the third floor of the sciences building." My mouth gaped!

I wasn't even sure what that meant. My research into technology-mediated course delivery began at that very moment.

Teleconferencing was a new medium for me and the students. The university had decided to extend its reach and offer the graduate research methods course via teleconference, never done previously at this institution. The first thing I did was start looking for things familiar—to me and to the students. Email was used by some but was available to all; I arranged for all to be connected via email. My first blended design. But another need emerged from the twenty-plus students in the course. They all lived within commuting distance from the institution, and they wanted to meet me—in person! I checked with the course coordinator: No in-person sessions allowed! But the students were insistent, so we arranged a kickoff face-to-face session, my first (but not last) act of subversive education design.

The course was an experience to remember, for me and the students. We were in it together, and that purposeful community provided a rich, fertile ground for teaching and learning together. It wasn't called blended learning then, but in the tradition of good education, I used what was available to create an engaging, accessible, and meaningful experience *for and with the students*.

I've been working on student-centered, multimodal, community-based teaching and learning ever since.

NEW ROLES FOR TEACHERS AND LEARNERS

Relationality and interaction are considered by many as new elements of the higher-education teaching and learning transaction. They previously existed as memorable moments of meaningful exchange, the occasional times when instructors actually saw a learner as a person, in evidence through conversation or feedback. I have an example. When I wrote my first paper in my first research methods course in graduate school, the prof responded: "Marti, you have captured all the issues, summarized the experts well, and even identified the critical elements for a practical approach. But *what do you think?*" It took me days to figure out what he meant. That I could take a stand and speak out was incomprehensible to a young female, raised in an academically oriented masculine household where there was little room for debate. He pushed all of us by asking "What does that mean?" "What do you mean?" "What else is there?" and "How do you know?" These memorable moments of individualized, interactive, and relational exchanges added significantly to my role as a learner, and ultimately shaped my role as a teacher. Now, this type of engagement is required not only in graduate school, but across the spectrum of learning.

These role requirements of teachers and learners can evolve to encourage deep learning through focused attention, reflection, and heightened awareness. Adjustment of each role, and its responsibilities—and requirements—can be considered through the lens of Garrison's concept of teach*ing* presence. Teaching presence allows each member of the course community varying degrees of responsibility in shaping the course. While the teacher of record remains the leader, the content expert, and the assessor of learning outcomes, learners are encouraged to reflect on and shape community activities. Adding to the role of learner, this shared obligation of supporting and shaping participant activities and the management of the course engages learners in a significant way.

Being the open, humble teacher as suggested by Thomas and Thorpe is the foundation for the constructed role of teacher through the co-construction of the course.[3] Rather than a bounded focus on the course content, teachers can lead the course-creation experience with the learners, allowing for shaping of materials, schedules, and activities in a collaborative, engaging way. For this to occur, teacher presence includes a leadership function as part of their role, focusing on leading learning processes rather than strictly acting as a content expert. The value of teach*ing* presence comes from moving beyond teach*er* presence to encouraging learner presence through a shared, collaborative set of activities.

To move both the learners and me, in my role as teacher, into a space of relationships and interaction, processes known to foster presence must be discussed, shaped, agreed to, and supported. It is in this combination of activities, through teacher presence and learner presence, that much relating and interacting can occur. My list of activities includes:

- providing structured activities that encourage and support interaction;
- facilitation of developing relationships through the sharing of thoughts, feelings, and interpretations;
- discussions of presence, its value to learning, and setting norms for social and cognitive interaction;
- moving from individual presentation of ideas through to paired interaction and group work;
- making explicit the value of critical reflection and collaborative learning; and
- accepting learner suggestions to add to course content and learning activities to share the role of teacher.

I perceive that my teacher and teaching presence roles, supported by the actions identified above, and others, offer interaction and relationality. Evidence that this may be so is seen here. A student once made this comment (paraphrased to ensure anonymity) about me in an online course evaluation: "Having you as an online teacher was akin to being called to dinner by one's grandmother; you knew it would be worth it to come and that the person calling would really be there when you arrived."

Hence, being not only present but present through interaction and relationality offers, according to this student, a warm sense of connectedness. This can support learning journeys in a number of ways, but more important for this vignette is to suggest that warm connectedness allows for the sense of safety necessary for the practice of contemplative pedagogies. In brief, Barbezat and Bush provide a focus on both teaching and learning presence, required when one speaks of pedagogy.[4] From their contemplative lens, teaching practices and learning requirements must seek to encourage deep learning through focused attention, reflection, and heightened awareness. They suggest that deep content engagement through contemplation and critical reflection leads to deep learning. Contemplative teaching, as defined by Byrnes, "creates space for learning and is a model of education that links the inner and external life in meaningful, transformative ways."[5]

My practical teaching experiences and academic study have led me to recognize that a move to contemplative teaching is built upon the safety created by shared teacher and learner presence: teaching presence. Staying the open, humble teacher as suggested by Thomas and Thorpe,[6] we must use this teaching presence so it can be shared with the learners. Rather than a bounded but deep, contemplative focus on the course content, teachers can lead the course-creation experience with the learners, allowing for shaping of materials, schedules, and activities in a collaborative, deeply engaging way. The value of teach*ing* presence comes from moving beyond teacher presence to encouraging learner presence through a shared, collaborative, contemplative set of activities.

NOTES

1. International Commission on the Futures of Education, "Reimagining Our Futures Together: A New Social Contract for Education; Executive Summary—UNESCO Digital Library" (Paris: UNESCO, 2021), https://unesdoc.unesco.org/ark:/48223/pf0000379381.

2. Glyn Thomas and Stephen Thorpe, "Enhancing the Facilitation of Online Groups in Higher Education: A Review of the Literature on Face-to-Face and Online Group-Facilitation," *Interactive Learning Environments* 27, no. 1 (2019): 67, doi:10.1080/10494820.2018.1451897.

3. Ibid.

4. Daniel Barbezat and Mirabai Bush, *Contemplative Practices in Higher Education: Powerful Methods to Transform Teaching and Learning*, Jossey-Bass Higher and Adult Education Series (San Francisco, CA: Jossey-Bass, 2014).

5. Kathryn Byrnes, "A Portrait of Contemplative Teaching: Embracing Wholeness," *Journal of Transformative Education* 10, no. 1 (2012): 37, doi:10.1177/1541344612456431.

6. Thomas and Thorpe, "Enhancing the Facilitation of Online Groups in Higher Education."

BIBLIOGRAPHY

Barbezat, Daniel, and Mirabai Bush. *Contemplative Practices in Higher Education: Powerful Methods to Transform Teaching and Learning*. Jossey-Bass Higher and Adult Education Series. San Francisco: Jossey-Bass, 2014.

Byrnes, Kathryn. "A Portrait of Contemplative Teaching: Embracing Wholeness." *Journal of Transformative Education* 10, no. 1 (2012): 22–41. doi:10.1177/1541344612456431.

International Commission on the Futures of Education. "Reimagining Our Futures Together: A New Social Contract for Education; Executive Summary—UNESCO Digital Library." Paris: UNESCO, 2021. https://unesdoc.unesco.org/ark:/48223/pf0000379381.

Thomas, Glyn, and Stephen Thorpe. "Enhancing the Facilitation of Online Groups in Higher Education: A Review of the Literature on Face-to-Face and Online Group-Facilitation." Interactive Learning Environments 27, no. 1 (2019): 62–71. doi:10.1080/10494820.2018.1451897.

Chapter Five

Grounding Presence

Beholding the Vulnerability of Emergency Remote Teaching and Learning

Karen Robert

Most of the contributions to this volume address the possibilities of integrating contemplative approaches into online teaching to foster a sense of presence in the virtual learning space. The authors share both theoretical and pragmatic insights into how educators can build online learning communities that help students to develop greater self-awareness, compassion for their fellow learners, and openhearted engagement with course material. However, the practices described here are not simply teaching "techniques" to be added to one's instructional toolkit; a foundational tenet of contemplative pedagogy is that this quality of presence must begin with the educator or facilitator. Before we can expect students to be vulnerable with each other and open themselves up to a fully embodied experience of learning, we must undertake our own contemplative practice to cultivate those qualities in ourselves.

While this suggestion may sound like yet another task to be added to our endless to-do lists, the good news is that contemplative practice can be enormously healing for professional academics. It can even feel like an act of rebellion to deliberately slow down and check in with ourselves in the face of neoliberal pressures to be productive at all times.[1] This is especially true in the current global context of escalating technological change and social and ecological breakdown, all of which are making it ever more difficult for us to remain balanced and for our students to learn and thrive. As I aim to demonstrate here, the cultivation of presence, including the ability to be present with our own unpleasant feelings and anxieties, can help academics navigate the uncertainties of the online space. It can also strengthen our confidence, so that we may carry that sense of groundedness into our interactions with our students and help them thrive in the face of adversity.

I would like to share the story here of my own evolution toward contemplative pedagogy, not as an "expert," but as an ordinary academic who gradually found ways to integrate my personal yoga and meditation practices into my professional life. After turning to these traditions some twenty years ago, I began experimenting with contemplative approaches to teaching over the past decade. More recently, I tried to bring a quality of contemplative leadership to my work as the remote teaching coordinator at my small, liberal arts campus during the forced transition to emergency remote teaching in 2020. In that role, I not only helped to advise the university on the necessary upgrades and training to move our campus online, but I offered myself as a sounding board for faculty and students, holding space for their anxieties and frustrations to encourage a culture of resilience at our institution.

A PERSONAL PRACTICE

I first came to yoga and mindfulness as an overwhelmed junior faculty member trying to balance my first tenure-track job with my role as mother to two young neurodivergent children. My kids, who are thriving young adults today, were creative, bright, and affectionate, but also easily frustrated and prone to wild temper tantrums. They had difficulties building stable friendships, and they needed a great deal of support to regulate their emotions and sensory experiences. Home had to be a safe space where they could let loose their energy, vent their frustrations, and be themselves. My husband and I did our best, but we struggled to provide that consistent space of calm while also managing work, extended family responsibilities, and financial challenges. We felt exhausted and isolated.

In 2003, a friend offered me a miraculous healing gift: a voucher for ten yoga classes at a studio within walking distance of my house. It was an extravagance I would not have paid for myself, but it laid the foundation for a yoga practice I have maintained more or less consistently ever since. Each week, those yoga classes helped me release accumulated stress, get in touch with my own body and mind, and recover a sense of purpose. I noticed that they also made me a wiser and more patient parent. They brought me back to myself.

As a professional researcher, of course I also turned to the library for help, and parenting books gave me some of my earliest training in mindful communication and self-awareness. The bestselling *How to Talk So Kids Will Listen & Listen So Kids Will Talk* provided scripts for active listening and intentional speech that still inform my personal and professional interactions.[2] The book *Parenting from the Inside Out*, by psychiatrist and mindfulness advocate Dr. Daniel Siegel and child-development expert Mary Hartzell, offered tools to help parents weather the ups and downs of family life and attune deeply with their children.³ They encouraged the same kinds of introspective practices I had encountered at yoga, explaining the science behind their benefits to the parent–child relationship. At the same time, they did not push parents to impose formal mindfulness practices on their family members, but instead to focus on strengthening their own self-awareness and emotional regulation to provide an anchor for their children's strong feelings.

Some of the most powerful insights I gained in these years came from writings about the neurobiology of attachment and attunement: the human capacity to connect with another person at a neurological level. Books by Daniel Goleman, Gordon Neufeld, and Gabor Maté taught me more about the functions of mirror neurons in the human brain.⁴ Discovered by scientists only in 1980, mirror neurons fire in our brains to "mirror" the internal states of the people around us; they help us sense what others are feeling even at an unconscious level. Yet such attunement is also deeply situational, fluctuating according to practice and circumstances. When we are rushed or stressed, we are also more likely to be distracted and disconnected from those around us. When we slow down and give someone our full attention, we are more able to pick up on their state of being and thus increase our capacity for empathy. This discovery provided a neuroscientific basis to ancient contemplative teachings about interconnectedness and the possibility of cultivating compassion through intentional practice.

As a parent of two children with strong feelings, I had the opportunity to practice the power of attunement every day. A therapist working with my family suggested that I view my highly sensitive children as a gift, because they served as finely tuned barometers for my own internal states. When the adults in our household were overwhelmed, distracted, or stressed, the children would manifest that stress through their own hyperactivity, tantrums, and difficulties sleeping. If we could stay calm and grounded, we could channel that calmness and help them settle.

"Mirroring" could also work with positive emotions. If one of my children was overflowing with excitement that felt like too much to handle, the best way to respond was not to insist that they calm down but to share in their feelings. For instance, if a child asked for an expensive item like a bicycle that I could not afford, the therapist suggested I simply validate their enthusiasm and give it some space: "Wouldn't that be fun? What's the most incredible bike you can imagine?" It worked better than any other parenting advice I had encountered. By meeting my kids where they were and holding space for their strong feelings, I could help those emotions move through them and dissipate.

Encouraged, I continued to read, practice, and expand my training over the years. I noticed how regular yoga improved my interoception: my ability to sense the internal state of my body.⁵ As I slowed down and paid attention to my breathing or to points of muscle tension, I became more attuned to my mental states and stress levels. A mindfulness-based stress reduction (MBSR) course introduced me to evidence-based practices like body scan meditation, which strengthened my tolerance for unpleasant physical sensations, thoughts, and emotions. These methods made me more aware of my own reactivity and less likely to slip into autopilot when facing stressful situations.

I also benefited from online guided meditations and talks by leading American psychologist and meditation teacher Tara Brach. I found a particularly useful resource in her RAIN practice, which she describes as "an easy-to-remember tool for bringing mindfulness and compassion to emotional difficulty."[6] Pema Chödrön's *When Things Fall Apart* and Jon Kabat-Zinn's *Full Catastrophe Living* delivered more valuable lessons about how to live a full life while being open to the truth that pain and unpredictability are unavoidable parts of the human condition.[7] All these teachings came with guided mindfulness and compassion practices that expanded my capacity to bring an open attitude or "beginner's mind" to the challenges of daily life, to create space for strong feelings and sensations, and attune to myself and those around me.

A MINDFUL TEACHING PRESENCE

I soon became curious about how I might integrate what I was learning into my undergraduate teaching. Like any teacher, I knew I could pick up on the energy in my classroom; on a given day, one group of students might feel energized while others radiated stress or fatigue. I also knew that feeling of unspoken connection when I "clicked" with my students and felt a sense of shared purpose or resonance in the classroom. Based on my rudimentary understanding of mirror neurons and attunement, I felt certain that there must be a way to cultivate such connections with greater intention. Moreover, I could see how stress, emotional difficulties, and distractions were undermining my students' ability to learn, and I wondered whether a mindful approach to teaching would help them.

One random classroom experiment from roughly a decade ago confirmed my intuitions. I entered my Introduction to World History classroom one day in the middle of the fall semester, prepared to administer a reading quiz. I could feel the buzz of anxiety in the room. The assigned chapter was challenging, and the students looked panicked. It was also just after the Canadian Thanksgiving break, a time when many of our first-year students suffer a wave of homesickness just as they head into the midterm crunch. On a whim, I invited them to take out a paper and freewrite an anonymous response to the prompt: "How are you doing, right here, right now?" I told them to take a few minutes to check in with themselves and write quickly about their physical, mental, and/or emotional states.

When I read over their responses while they worked on their quizzes, I was shocked. Out of over one hundred students, only about ten described an overall sense of well-being. The others expressed overwhelming feelings of despair, anxiety, and loneliness. They described illness, financial hardships, worries about family members, and so on. When I commented to the group: "Most of you are having a really hard time, aren't you?" several of my students had tears in their eyes. They felt seen and heard, and each of them realized that they were not alone.

I responded to this situation first by cutting material from my syllabus and slowing down the pace of the course. I also decided to send my students out for a tech-free walk at our next meeting. My instructions were for them to walk around our beautiful campus or the surrounding streets by themselves for about twenty minutes. I did not use the words *mindfulness* or *meditation*, but I did ask them to leave their phones and backpacks behind and to just take in the experience of walking and noticing their surroundings. I had them respond again to the same prompt when they returned, and several described the experience as a revelation. Some noted it had been years since they had spent even twenty minutes detached from their phones, and others could not remember the last time they had spent time outside for no reason. Many noticed a complete change in their mental state; though they still had just as much work to do, they felt better equipped to face it. Several mentioned the experience on their final course evaluations, and one student told me in her graduating year that just that simple walk had prompted her to change her postgraduation plans and pursue a career that allowed her to work outside.

EMBODIMENT

Buoyed by this success, in 2013 I jumped at the chance to attend a weeklong "Mindfulness in Education" retreat led by the Vietnamese Zen master and peace activist Thich Nhat Hanh as part of his Plum Village community's Wake Up Schools initiative.[8] Some 1,300 participants practiced daily walking and sitting meditations, mindful movement classes, and silent mealtimes, while also attending workshops and presentations about how to incorporate mindfulness into our teaching. The main lesson shared in the teachings and the example provided by "Thay" himself was the same one I had learned in the parenting literature: The best way to be a mindful teacher is to cultivate a grounded presence in myself. In the Plum Village tradition, this core principle of "embodiment" acknowledges that "our greatest teaching is the presence that we offer to others; we seek first to embody a peaceful, happy presence, so that we can be truly there for our students and our educational community."[9]

I came back from the Plum Village retreat anxious to connect with other university educators who shared my interests, since most attendees had been from the K–12 sector. I had been placed in a small discussion group with other postsecondary professionals, but most of them worked in counseling and student services. The handful of other academics hailed from fields like theater and social work that seemed better suited to contemplative approaches that incorporate introspection, body work, ethics, and deep practices of mindful dialogue. As a professor of history, I belong instead to a discipline that privileges analytical thinking above all other forms of knowing: a field where students are taught to read texts and artifacts critically and to express themselves logically.

My years of personal mindfulness and yoga practice had made me question this detached approach, especially since I recognized that the content students encounter in their history courses can easily contribute to their distress and feelings of helplessness. My own students confront disturbing topics such as slavery, colonialism, and the historic roots of the current environmental crisis in my classroom. As a parent, I am cognizant that this learning comes at a delicate period in their lives when they are forming their identities as adults and are especially vulnerable to mental health difficulties. As an instructor, I also came to realize that conventional teaching methods gave my students little space for any feelings that might arise through their learning.

My time with the Plum Village community made me reconsider my professional relationship with my students and the material we study together. Though still committed to the goal of helping them become well-informed citizens of the world, which includes teaching them about difficult subjects, I became more concerned with helping them to find meaning in that learning. Yet as I dug into the best pedagogical literature about the teaching of history, I found no guidance about how to help students process or reflect upon the deeper, more human implications of this knowledge.[10] Though I encountered much innovative and valuable scholarship, the methods for teaching human history still struck me as paradoxically devoid of human emotion and connection.

The next turning point in my training came in 2018, when I attended the 14th Annual Summer Session on Contemplative Learning hosted by the Center for Contemplative Mind in Society. There I encountered dozens of other academics, including some from "hard" analytical disciplines like political science, law, and chemistry, who shared my values and preoccupations. These were university professors with a strong commitment to social justice education who also believed that learning should engage the whole person, including that person's body, senses, feelings, and intuitions. Even more striking was the fact that these academics recognized that they had bodies! Unlike any other academic gathering I had attended, there were opportunities for sitting meditation, morning yoga, and creative workshops along with formal talks and presentations. Presenters modeled how they infused their own teaching with mindfulness and compassion through intentional pauses, rituals of "arrival" that welcomed students into the shared learning space, and activities that fostered deep listening and empathy. I had found a community of like-minded scholars and educators that I didn't even know existed.

Of course, this embracing of vulnerability and compassionate "presence" runs counter to mainstream academic culture, even though contemplative approaches to teaching have gained ground on university campuses. In a deeply competitive profession, academics are socialized to take themselves seriously. They are taught to defend their reputations at all costs, and to project an air of competence at all times: to be "bulletproof," in the words of one commentator.[11] This professional culture makes it extremely risky for faculty to share any personal vulnerabilities, and the professional costs can be high for those who need accommodation for physical or mental health challenges or family responsibilities. In short, as early as graduate school, academics learn that they could commit professional suicide by bringing their "whole selves" to work. These pressures have only been compounded in recent years by budget cuts, precarious employment, and management accountability measures, all of which have contributed to high levels of stress and burnout among university professors.[12]

COVID-19 AND EMERGENCY REMOTE TEACHING

When the COVID-19 crisis shut down campuses around the world in 2020, university professors suddenly found themselves forced into a state of acute vulnerability, forced to learn new technologies and new teaching modalities under extreme time pressures. Faculty who had only taught face-to-face were often skeptical about the value of online learning, but they did not have time to engage with the ample literature on distance education. As they rushed to redesign their courses and learn new skills, many reported feelings of helplessness and frustration. They also worried about their students, feared for their jobs and the future of their institutions, and struggled to manage their own family responsibilities and health concerns related to the pandemic. One Canadian study found that professors characterized their work lives under COVID-19 as a cycle of "never-ending repetitiveness, sadness, loss, [and] 'juggling with a blindfold on.'"[13]

I had a unique perspective on the faculty experience of emergency remote teaching at my own institution in 2020–2021. I teach at a small, publicly funded liberal arts college in New Brunswick, one of Canada's poorest and most rural provinces. My institution prides itself on its tight-knit campus community and small class sizes, and our student body includes many non-traditional students who are the first in their families to attend university. They come from small towns, Indigenous communities, or rural areas with poor Internet service and limited access to technology. A smaller cohort of international students hail from several Latin American, Asian, and African countries. A significant minority of our students qualify for learning accommodations, and most are struggling to pay for their education, taking out loans and working long hours while they are in school.

It has been a privilege for me to work at such a unique institution for over twenty years, boosting young people's confidence in their ability to learn and opening them up to the wider world. However, the unique qualities of our campus also made us especially vulnerable when COVID-19 hit. The focus on face-to-face relationships meant that the university offered no online classes, and many faculty had never even learned to use Moodle, our learning management system. We had no instructional designers or educational technology specialists on staff either.

I happened to occupy the role of acting learning and teaching officer when classes were forced online in March 2020, and I worked with our information technology staff to cobble together some basic resources to help faculty finish the semester online. In the process, I quickly came to the alarming realization that I was one of the more tech-savvy instructors on our campus. I joked that we had about four months over the summer of 2020 to drag the entire institution from the nineteenth century into the twenty-first.

Seeing the monumental challenge we faced, I (perhaps foolishly) offered to take up a new ad hoc position to advise the administration on preparations for emergency remote teaching. Though I was by no means an expert, I was at least comfortable with technology, in part because my husband had been working for several years in educational technology at another institution. I also had good people skills and an ability to bridge communications between faculty and the IT staff. For the next twelve months, I worked with an advisory committee comprised of representatives from faculty, students, the information technology and student services departments, and other administrative offices on campus. Together we researched hardware and software upgrades, wrote grant applications, advised the administration on hiring new training staff, and surveyed staff and students regarding their needs.

My main role, however, was as a liaison and a sounding board for faculty. From my interactions with panicked colleagues in those last weeks of the

2019–2020 academic year, I sensed that faculty needed a reassuring presence to help them navigate the immense challenges they were facing. I thought there was a place for a "neutral" figure to support them outside the adversarial framework of labor relations, because I knew that our extremely competent faculty union would take care of defending our workplace interests. I intuited that I might be the right person to provide that grounding presence since I had worked at the institution for roughly two decades and had generally positive relationships with colleagues. I also had the confidence to take on new challenges around technology, and I was not a member of upper administration, which meant I had no real power or interest in "managing" people.

It was only in retrospect that I realized how much this new role had grown out of my years of contemplative practice, including the work that I had done with my own children and my students. I knew from personal experience and from my readings in mindfulness and neuroscience that faculty would not be able to learn a host of new skills and navigate new uncertainties from a place of reactivity. Though I could not solve the overall crisis, I could try to help those who were struggling by acting as an anchor and holding space for their strong feelings. In one-on-one meetings, I listened while colleagues vented about their frustrations, helplessness, and cognitive fatigue. Overwhelmed by the demands of learning new ways of working, many reported feelings of incompetence, like they had been stripped of all their expertise and returned to their first year of teaching. What they were describing was a raw experience of vulnerability that ran absolutely counter to their professional socialization.

Faculty were also deeply worried about their students, whose personal lives had been laid bare by the crisis. During the full lockdown, students who relied on free Wi-Fi on campus or in coffee shops couldn't even get online. Some had to start working full-time or move home because their parents had lost employment, while others were caregiving or facing their own extra health risks. Faculty who opted for synchronous teaching through Teams or Zoom because they thought it would most resemble classroom instruction found themselves facing a screen of icons as students resisted turning on their cameras. Many instructors reported feeling utterly unqualified to help their students in these circumstances. How could they reach out to a student who seemed to be in crisis if they were living off campus? How could they offer the appropriate attitude of care and compassion? Messages from upper administration urging patience and accommodation only deepened some instructors' feelings of helplessness.

Since such feelings had no place in academic culture, people often expressed themselves in the first instance through the more sanctioned emotions of anger and outrage. They might rail against the messaging coming from upper administration, complain about the IT staff, or react defensively to suggestions they learn new teaching methods. I knew from experience that this kind of "complaint culture" could fracture our tight-knit learning community because, years earlier, a faculty lockout and strike had fostered toxic rumors and deeply damaged trust on our campus.

When speaking with colleagues, I did my best to hold space for these strong feelings without giving advice, following lessons on mindful communication taught at the retreats I had attended.[14] Instead, I offered my own grounded presence so that people would feel heard. I tried to bring a calm, reassuring attitude to all my professional encounters that year, whether I was meeting with the advisory committee, holding virtual office hours with students, or hosting a town hall to inform faculty about our progress. When I listened attentively, I found that I could let people vent until their anger dissipated and they admitted to feeling overwhelmed by a situation that they recognized was out of everyone's control. When I hosted virtual town hall meetings as a faculty colleague, I provided space for people to air their grievances while gently countering rumors and negativity.

Sometimes people contacted me in a rage because they could not master some new technological skill. Since I knew that our IT personnel were just as overwhelmed as faculty, I let them vent their anger and frustration until they were calm enough to ask for help in a civil manner. If the matter was simple enough, I might be able to solve it myself. If not, I could direct them to the proper person, help them find the right language to phrase their request, and remind them that everyone was pulling in the same direction. When colleagues admitted to feeling helpless and incompetent, I would hear them out and eventually offer a gentle reminder that they were experts in their own fields, and they still had the same mastery over their course content.

One person with whom I shared a long-standing professional relationship began the summer of 2020 in full-blown reactivity, convinced that more than twenty-five years of teaching experience were suddenly worthless. Yet they gradually came around to an attitude of openness and acceptance, a willingness to learn from the training professionals we had hired. They engaged deeply with new approaches to teaching and even immersed themselves in the literature on trauma-informed pedagogy, which has continued to shape their teaching as we have returned to in-person teaching. Several other colleagues messaged me with expressions of gratitude after the town hall meetings I hosted, and to this day people continue to thank me and the other members of the committee for all the work we did. They say that we made a terrible year somewhat more bearable, and they appreciated the positive, can-do attitude we brought to the challenges of upgrading our campus.

Finally, lest I appear to be casting myself as an enlightened being, I should clarify that I was able to maintain this equanimity during the 2020–2021 year because I was hardly teaching. My heavy administrative responsibilities meant that I taught only one course, and I was already working so closely with our new educational technologist that I simply followed her advice to the letter and adapted it to asynchronous delivery. I was not in the trenches like so many of my colleagues, who were teaching two or three courses each semester. The following winter, in fact, I noticed myself exhibiting the exact same stress reactions when our campus reopened, and we had to use hybrid methods to accommodate both in-person and remote learners. I was just as overwhelmed when the equipment wouldn't work in the first five minutes of class, just as discouraged when I felt disconnected from students who were trying to learn from home because they had COVID-19. My years of practice provided some comfort, however, at least in those moments when I remembered to take a breath, step back, notice my own reactions, and smile at the absurdity of the human condition.

The compounding crises of our current world—COVID-19, lockdowns, warfare, the climate crisis, political polarization, social justice struggles—have brought to the fore our vulnerability and interconnectedness. As other contributors to this volume have stressed, it is time for university educators to acknowledge this vulnerability in our own lives, and to make space for it in our classrooms and institutions, both in person and online. That prospect is daunting—even frightening. Thankfully, deep wisdom traditions exist that can help us find strength to navigate uncertainty, so that we, in turn, can act as anchors for our students.

NOTES

1. Maggie Berg and Barbara K. Seeber, *The Slow Professor: Challenging the Culture of Speed in the Academy* (Toronto: University of Toronto Press, 2016).

2. Adele Faber and Elaine Mazlish, *How to Talk So Kids Will Listen & Listen So Kids Will Talk* (New York: Scribner, 2012).

3. Daniel Siegel and Mary Hartzell, *Parenting from the Inside Out: How a Deeper Self-Understanding Can Help You Raise Children Who Thrive*, 10th Anniversary Edition (New York: TarcherPerigee, 2013).

4. Daniel Goleman, *Emotional Intelligence: Why It Can Matter More Than IQ* (New York: Bantam Books, 2005); Gabor Maté, *Scattered Minds: The Origins and Healing of Attention Deficit Disorder* (Toronto: Vintage Canada, 2000); Gordon Neufeld and Gabor Maté, *Hold On to Your Kids: Why Parents Need to Matter More than Peers* (Toronto: Knopf Canada, 2013).

5. For a fascinating discussion of recent neuroscientific research into interoception and other forms of bodily knowing, see Annie Murphy Paul, *The Extended Mind: The Power of Thinking Outside the Brain* (Boston: Houghton Mifflin Harcourt, 2021).

6. Tara Brach, "RAIN: A Practice of Radical Compassion," January 1, 2020, https://www.tarabrach.com/rain-practice-radical-compassion/ (accessed October 6, 2022). She also offers resources for new meditators at https://www.tarabrach.com/new-to-meditation/.

7. Pema Chödron, *When Things Fall Apart: Heart Advice for Difficult Times*, 20th Anniversary Edition (Boulder, CO: Shambhala, 2016); Jon Kabat-Zinn, *Full Catastrophe Living: How to Cope with Stress, Pain, and Illness Using Mindfulness Meditation* (London: Piatkus, 2013).

8. Wake Up Schools, https://wakeupschools.org/.

9. "What Is Wake Up Schools?" https://wakeupschools.org/about-us/what-is-wake-up-schools/ (accessed October 6, 2022). Thich Nhat Hanh's students commonly refer to him as *Thay*, the Vietnamese word for "teacher."

10. See, for example, the excellent work being done by the Stanford History Education Group, https://sheg.stanford.edu/ (accessed October 18, 2022); Sam Weinberg, *Historical Thinking and Other Unnatural Acts: Charting the Future of Teaching the Past* (Philadelphia: Temple University Press, 2012).

11. Anonymous. "The Invisible Injuries of Faculty Mental Health." *Inside Higher Ed*, August 31, 2018, https://www.insidehighered.com/advice/2018/08/31/removing-stigma-faculty-members-mental-health-disorders-opinion.

12. Holly Else, "Academics 'Face Higher Mental Health Risk' than Other Professions," *The Times Higher Education*, August 22, 2017, https://www.timeshighereducation.com/news/academics-face-higher-mental-health-risk-than-other-professions (accessed September 10, 2022); Rebecca Pope-Ruark, *Unraveling Faculty Burnout: Pathways to Reckoning and Renewal* (Baltimore: Johns Hopkins University Press, 2022).

13. Charlene A. VanLeeuwen et al., "Never-Ending Repetitiveness, Sadness, Loss, and 'Juggling with a Blindfold On': Lived Experiences of Canadian College and University Faculty Members during the COVID-19 Pandemic," *British Journal of Educational Technology* 52, no. 4 (2021): 1306–22. See also Bram Bruggeman et al., "Exploring University Teachers' Online Education During COVID-19: Tensions Between Enthusiasm and Stress," *Computers and Education Open*, 3 (2022): 1–13; P. C. Pradeepkumar et al., "Depression, Anxiety and Stress Among College Faculties During the COVID-19 Pandemic," *Indian Journal of Health & Wellbeing* 12, no 4 (December 2021): 470–73.

14. For an excellent introduction to mindful communication, see Oren Jay Sofer, *Say What You Mean: A Mindful Approach to Nonviolent Communication* (Boulder, CO: Shambhala, 2018).

BIBLIOGRAPHY

Anonymous. "The Invisible Injuries of Faculty Mental Health." *Inside Higher Ed*, August 31, 2018. https://www.insidehighered.com/advice/2018/08/31/removing-stigma-faculty-members-mental-health-disorders-opinion.

Berg, Maggie, and Barbara K. Seeber. *The Slow Professor: Challenging the Culture of Speed in the Academy*. Toronto: University of Toronto Press, 2016.

Brach, Tara. "RAIN: A Practice of Radical Compassion." January 1, 2020, https://www.tarabrach.com/rain-practice-radical-compassion/ (accessed October 6, 2022).

Bruggeman, Bram, et al. "Exploring University Teachers' Online Education During COVID-19: Tensions Between Enthusiasm and Stress." *Computers and Education Open*, 3 (2022): 1–13.

Chödron, Pema. *When Things Fall Apart: Heart Advice for Difficult Times*. 20th anniversary edition. Boulder, CO: Shambhala, 2016.

Else, Holly. "Academics 'Face Higher Mental Health Risk' than Other Professions." *The Times Higher Education*, August 22, 2017.

Faber, Adele, and Elaine Mazlish. *How to Talk So Kids Will Listen & Listen So Kids Will Talk*. New York: Scribner, 2012.

Goleman, Daniel. *Emotional Intelligence: Why It Can Matter More Than IQ*. New York: Bantam Books, 2005.

Kabat-Zinn, Jon. *Full Catastrophe Living: How to Cope with Stress, Pain, and Illness Using Mindfulness Meditation*. London: Piatkus, 2013.

Maté, Gabor. *Scattered Minds: The Origins and Healing of Attention Deficit Disorder*. Toronto: Vintage Canada, 2000.

Neufeld, Gordon, and Gabor Maté. *Hold On to Your Kids: Why Parents Need to Matter More Than Peers*. Toronto: Knopf Canada, 2013.

Paul, Annie Murphy *The Extended Mind: The Power of Thinking Outside the Brain*. Boston: Houghton Mifflin Harcourt, 2021.

Pope-Ruark, Rebecca. *Unraveling Faculty Burnout: Pathways to Reckoning and Renewal*. Baltimore: Johns Hopkins University Press, 2022.

Pradeepkumar, P. C., et al. "Depression, Anxiety and Stress among College Faculties during the COVID-19 Pandemic." *Indian Journal of Health & Wellbeing* 12, no. 4 (December 2021): 470–73.

Siegel, Daniel, and Mary Hartzell. *Parenting from the Inside Out: How a Deeper Self-Understanding Can Help You Raise Children Who Thrive*. 10th anniversary edition. New York: TarcherPerigee, 2013.

Sofer, Oren Jay. *Say What You Mean: A Mindful Approach to Nonviolent Communication*. Boulder, CO: Shambhala, 2018.

VanLeeuwen, Charlene A., et al. "Never-Ending Repetitiveness, Sadness, Loss, and 'Juggling with a Blindfold On': Lived Experiences of Canadian College and University Faculty Members during the COVID-19 Pandemic." *British Journal of Educational Technology* 52, no. 4 (2021): 1306–22.

Wake Up Schools. https://wakeupschools.org/.

Weinberg, Sam. *Historical Thinking and Other Unnatural Acts: Charting the Future of Teaching the Past*. Philadelphia: Temple University Press, 2012.

Chapter Six

Vignette 2

Presence and Silence in the Virtual Classroom

Margaret Anne Smith

How do we cultivate presence and connection through real silence in a virtual world? How do we "take a deep breath" in order to better listen, think, and engage with others? Unless we have preplanned our online teaching and learned specific techniques for the optimal virtual classroom experience, remote teaching and learning can descend into the tired format of lecture and passive observation, with student cameras off and very little human interaction. However, university life in a pandemic has offered me an important teaching and learning moment.

In late March of 2020, the COVID-19 pandemic became locally relevant and required us to empty campus and shift to "emergency remote learning." Like it did for most people around the globe, the shift to lockdown had both personal and professional consequences for me. In terms of my teaching alone, I was absolutely made dizzy by the array of tech options and systems and platforms offered—and even expected for our use. I love teaching and I love real classrooms, and the interplay of ideas and energies we get from learning together in a physical space. My teaching techniques are typically varied: some days are technology-dependent, and other days I simply work with a whiteboard and class is discussion-focused. The shift to emergency remote learning was overwhelming and disappointing to me. And my undergraduate daughter was suddenly living at home again, having the same disappointing experience in the next room, from a student point of view. We assumed this would be short-lived.

Having taken on a new administrative role the following year, I opted to teach one course, thinking campus life and learning would be back to normal. Teaching was the one thing I looked forward to every week. I planned a small seminar, with senior students in my field of modern and contemporary literature; what's not to love? Then pandemic reality set in for yet another term, and I realized I had two students learning remotely (with bad rural Internet), four present in my classroom, and two others who switched back and forth from real to remote whenever they felt they needed to. We used a not-always-reliable learning management system, and campus Wi-Fi wasn't strong enough for so much streaming. It often took ten to fifteen minutes out of the seventy-five-minute class to sort it all out. Every week. This kind of blended classroom—real plus virtual, in real time—felt like the worst of both worlds. The tech uncertainty of beginning each class had me rattled, distracted, and unfocused.

A technical breakdown helped me realize what was missing, and reminded me to refocus, slow down, ask questions, listen for answers, and encourage students to find ways to connect with each other, with me, and with our course material. One morning, one remote student (I'll call him Z) had enough Internet bandwidth at his rural home to hear us, but we couldn't see him and couldn't hear him consistently. With a small class of students, I was attempting the kind of discussion we would typically have when we are all in the same room. To participate, Z would laboriously type his comments in the chat function, but by the time he had typed something up and I had noticed his words in the chat box, we had moved on in our discussion. Partway through the class, noticing the ". . ." in the chat box that indicated Z was typing, I said to the class, "Let's just wait; everyone hold on, think for a bit, write down some thoughts, and give Z a chance to catch up." This simple pause changed everything. One student actually typed "ooooooh silence. weeeeeird" in the chat box.

I have frequently used silence to create space in real classrooms: using a mindfulness practice like focused breathing to help us all settle in at the beginning of class; allowing time for in-class journaling and silent reading; reading aloud with the class, then pausing; taking them outdoors for walking and observing sessions, etc. Giving one student quiet time to catch up on his two-fingered typing made me realize I had been caught up in the tech struggles, and had lapsed back into filling the silence with lectures—a type of teaching I hadn't done for twenty years. I felt like a brand-new teacher, and forgot the things that I knew about presence and connection. I was obsessing about getting the tech right, and stuck on content delivery.

I'm really grateful that the tech glitch happened for Z early in the term. It was the reminder for me to figure out how to create space virtually. I invited people to take turns speaking, or to pass. I created silent spaces in the middle of class for thinking/writing/processing, and invited students to read those written reflections aloud, or to send those in-class reflections to me—or even better, to post and share them for all to see. And they did! They even started posting in our online forum on weekends—"Hey, have you read this poem?" "Here is a photo of the beach walk I took on the weekend!" "Hey, Z [or K or B], here's a reference you might like for your research paper." Their instincts for presence and compassion and connection shone, and they showed creativity and resilience. I just needed to create the space for these qualities to flourish.

I needed to calm down, and admit this to myself and my students. We spent more class time talking about how difficult life was in the COVID-19 pandemic, and how disappointed we were to be separated. This even helped us to better connect to the course content. We were reading Oscar Wilde, T. S. Eliot, Virginia Woolf, Langston Hughes, and Waubgeshig Rice, all of whom talk about hopelessness and the need for human connection. Throughout the term, students produced remarkable presentations and papers. We laughed and lamented together. For me, the course (tech glitches and all) became the highlight of a long year, and a humbling yet energizing experience in a long teaching career.

ALLOWING SILENCE IN CLASS

I frequently allow time for ten to fifteen minutes of silence in class.

For the first couple of weeks of a course, I explain that this practice helps everyone—particularly introverts, international students, and the neurodiverse—to process information and better participate in a variety of ways. (They can speak up later in class discussion, or give me—or post—their written thoughts.) It encourages writing as a tool for thinking; it gives people a chance to return to a text and reread; it offers a chance to reflect and articulate questions; it allows catch-up time to review a reading or notes; and sometimes it just offers a quiet oasis in a frantic day. When offered toward the end of the class time, quiet time encourages students to listen to others and evaluate what they have learned in that class. I often prompt: "What did you think about this topic before you attended class today? Now that class is almost over, having listened to a lecture or a discussion, what do you think now?"

This practice also normalizes silence, in an age in which there is so much noise. I ask students not to use headphones, and not to connect with the Internet during this time. They are sitting, reading, writing, thinking, reconsidering, or staring into space. All of these choices are good.

PAUSE

Look at a Plant Indoors or Outdoors Breathe Fully

Chapter Seven

Connection and Compassion
Presence Inside and Outside the Online Classroom[1]

Leslie Ann Jeffrey

The emergency remote classroom definitely challenged my ability to be present for, and connected to, my students. Classroom technology and learning systems were never something I had turned my attention to, and my entry into remote teaching was filled with dread and no small amount of panic. I had hoped that the students would be more comfortable with the technology, but I quickly discovered that they too were uncomfortable in this new space. Few turned on their cameras during class time—and then only rarely. It was often unclear whether they were actually there or not.

My strongest memory of this experience is of feeling—each time I started another synchronous online class—that I was facing a brick wall, blocking not only my connection to the students but my connection to myself and my own thinking and experience. Indeed, the surfeit of technological interfaces that marked this season of remote teaching took a huge cognitive toll as I navigated my way through these systems (which seemed to change constantly) in order to be able to communicate with my students. By the time I "arrived" in the online classroom I was already overwhelmed, confused, and cognitively exhausted. Being present was a big ask.

I was especially frustrated because it struck me that this was precisely the year in which we needed to be together, in the physical classroom, doing education differently through contemplative methods that would help us to reconnect in deep and meaningful ways in order to respond to the various crises we were facing, and to build a new world. I teach political science and international relations through such topics as human rights, gender politics, and Global North/South relations. The online classroom appeared to present a massive obstacle, contributing to further disengagement, isolation, and distraction. I was somewhat despairing of the possibilities for using contemplative pedagogy in this unfamiliar, and unwanted, context.

I teach in a small, urban, mainly undergraduate, campus, and distraction, overwhelm, and anxiety mark many of my students' lives. As a mainly commuter campus there is often little sense of connection to the university itself, and many view their degrees as necessary parts of the scramble for (hopefully decent) jobs, but also as a real challenge to undertake in their already overburdened and complicated lives. Our students are often drawn in several competing directions, including jobs and families; poverty and underemployment are a constant background threat. For all of these reasons, more technology seemed like a bad idea. Further, this overwhelm and distraction, the disconnection from "deep thought," presented a huge obstacle to addressing the obvious crises which we faced: the social, economic, political, and environmental inequities and injustices of our age. If there was ever a time in which we needed to be back in the classroom reestablishing connection, free from distractive and distancing technologies, I thought, this was it.

The year of emergency remote teaching, however, also opened up new possibilities in unexpected ways. The suddenness of the shift to online learning created a willingness to experiment, an understanding that we needed to be creative and flexible, and it therefore also created an openness to nontraditional methods like contemplative pedagogy. Though political science classes were often the last place students expected to find contemplative practices, they were surprisingly open to the idea. Moreover, in removing our usual reliance on physical proximity as a stand-in for presence, going remote made the work of establishing presence visible and comprehensible. Presence—connection and compassion, to ourselves and others—became more clearly something we have to build and strengthen, a muscle we can exercise, in whatever context we find ourselves. Finally, occurring as it did in a year of several profound crises, the shift to online learning created an openness to, and even a demand for, the kind of compassion and connection that defines presence, exactly what is called for in responding to these crises.

While we didn't articulate it this way at the time, looking back I can see that together my students and I began to develop a practice of presence through this challenging year. We discovered that being present in online teaching and learning did not necessarily always mean a synchronous online class. Instead, we used a series of individual contemplative practices designed to help us connect with ourselves, each other, and the Earth itself. Through these practices, we were all able to cultivate at least some sense of awareness, connection, and compassion—what I would consider the key components of true presence, and the foundation to helping students develop into resilient and compassionate humans who can build a better future.

PRESENCE: CONNECTION AND COMPASSION

My conceptualization of presence is very much informed by a sense of connection and the practice of compassion. Presence for me, as noted elsewhere in this collection, is relational. It is a simultaneously inward and outward attunement, a stillness that allows me to connect first with my own internal somatic, emotional, and intuitive experience in any given moment. In forging that connection to my own inner being, beyond the presentation of self and ego, I am then able to connect with, or at least reach toward—as through a thin electrified thread, or a mycelial network—this vulnerable inner core of others.[2]

This connection both seeds and is nested in compassion. To see someone else as "just like me" at that most basic human level facilitates this connection, and the connection enables the flow of warmth and acceptance, not only toward others, but also ourselves. The thread snaps when the connection becomes overly analytical and cold, and it is impossible to establish if we fail to approach our own inner selves with spaciousness and warmth. This dialectic of compassion and connection leads me to see these two forces as inseparable components of presence. As we engaged in practices of self-compassion and connection during this year of remote teaching and learning, what we were simultaneously cultivating was both my and their sense of presence.

Developing this sense of presence, of connection and compassion, is particularly important to me because of my commitment to teaching as a "practice of freedom," as bell hooks would have it.[3] My hope is for students to learn to challenge the way things are, and particularly the inequities and injustices that shape our world. As a practicing meditator for a decade, I had been deeply affected by how contemplative practices give us actual tools with which to create profound internal, and ultimately social, change. As a social scientist, I had long focused on the systemic or social level and eschewed the individual and internal (either as the terrain of psychology or the ground of neoliberalism). But years of contemplative study and practice made it clear how deeply interconnected the individual and societal levels are and how critical individual-level change is to wider social change.[4]

My drive to bring in contemplative methods took on a kind of urgency in this year of profound social upheaval, because of my growing conviction that contemplative approaches were absolutely vital to addressing the roots of these crises. At their root, the crises of racism, sexism, inequality, and climate change are founded in disconnection—from ourselves, each other, and the planet. And as Bai et al. have made clear, traditional modes of education have supported this divisive and disconnected worldview.[5] Developing presence, understood as connection and compassion, was, I felt, at the core of being able to address these social crises and the very reason for adopting contemplative pedagogy.

CONNECTING WITH SELF

"You can't connect with others if you can't connect with yourself" was a central motif of my years of contemplative training. Getting to know ourselves and becoming "our own best friends" was the ground from which all practices began, and so I initially started classes off with a self-compassion exercise that would, I hoped, help students to gain perspective on their own experiences and feelings. At the same time, I was keenly aware of the dangers of "McMindfulness," laid out by Ron Purser and David Forbes. Used merely as a stress-reduction exercise, students may simply learn to accommodate themselves to the structures causing that stress rather than challenging them and fighting for change.[6] However, being present to their own experience was a key first step in developing the resilience to face the challenges we all need to face in this era of crisis and overcoming the technological disconnect we all feel. Developing this kind of presence to oneself offline could contribute to our sense of connectedness online.

CONNECTING WITH OURSELVES

1. First, find a comfortable spot to sit where you can be without distractions, preferably outside. Bring writing material, but try to leave your technology behind. Take a moment just to relax into the space. Then bring your attention to how your body feels, to your breathing, to the feeling of just relaxing.
2. Now, start writing in response to the following prompts:

   - What has it been like for you in the time of COVID-19: the good, and the bad?
   - What has the start of term been like for you?
   - What might a good friend say to you if you were talking to them right now? Do you notice a difference in how this friend would talk to you and how you talk to yourself? (What kind of tone do they take, for example?)
   - How might things change for you if you talked to yourself like this friend?

3. Type up a one-page summary of how this experience was for you. What did you learn or observe about yourself?

Adapting Gemer and Neff's "How would you treat a friend" exercise, I had students find a time to sit (preferably outside) and write a simple reflection on the year so far and then switch perspective and imagine what a friend would say to them in response. Many spoke of their sense of anxiety and overwhelm, of their financial and emotional struggles through the pandemic. As predicted by Gemer and Neff, by taking the perspective of a good friend, a number recognized their tendency toward harsh self-talk and allowed that they deserved some empathy and compassion.[7] The imagined perspective of a friend created a compassionate context that enabled students to be present with their own suffering but not be overwhelmed by it. As David Kahane, who teaches global ethics, has pointed out elsewhere, what often leaves students unable to connect with others' suffering is the "inchoate fear" that allowing suffering to enter in will destroy them.[8] Thus, it is vital to learn to approach our own suffering in order to be able to connect with others, rather than remain indifferent to them. Of course, not every student found this an easy process. One found it simply too painful to engage in, and so I was reminded of the importance of trauma-informed approaches to all of these practices, and quickly negotiated alternatives for those for whom this was already a step too far.[9]

Importantly, the students did not get mired in self-pity as I had feared. Instead, they often reflected back on the social justice themes of the courses and recognized their own relative privilege. Furthermore, they expressed hope for a better collective future rather than falling back into a sense of nihilism and despair. For example, one student, after detailing a fairly difficult year during COVID-19, ended with this reflection: "I live in a largely unaffected part of the world in an upper-middle-class household. Many, however, have been far less lucky. I'm thankful every day to be where I am, and I hope the world comes out of this in a better state than it went in." Taking this kind of perspective is central to the self-compassion process, according to Neff, and it was certainly key to my hope that they see themselves in the context of the world around them.[10]

The students were also sometimes spurred to action, recognizing that their happiness was at least partly in their own hands. Many commented that they would start taking this time more often. Another stated: "This journal has gotten me to think about myself and what I need to do to make myself happier, and after writing this I am going to message a friend I haven't talked to in a while" This kind of incentive to action, this recognition of their capacity for change, also filled me with hope, since the field I teach in always teeters on the edge of inducing cynicism and giving up in the face of seemingly insurmountable obstacles. That they gained some sense that they could do something, no matter how small, to change things even in their own lives, was, I felt, an important step to building a sense of efficacy in the world.

Overall, the students deeply appreciated the opportunity to have the space and time to be present to themselves. For me, reading their stories helped me to see them as people with lives, beyond the icon on the screen that I interacted with in classes. They took the first steps toward being vulnerable and open about the reality of their lives.

CONNECTING WITH SELF AND/IN NATURE

Perhaps the most impactful way students were able to connect with themselves offline was in the nature-based exercises I introduced. Students were invited to take a mindful walk, preferably in a natural area, without their "tech," and pay close attention to their senses. Despite often inclement weather, many students were grateful for the "enforced" opportunity to get offline, and go outside. Many commented in these journals about how challenging they had found the remote classroom and the difficulty focusing they experienced when learning through a screen. Certainly, the walks made many of them feel more grounded, less stressed, and calmer.[11] There were also some indications of the development of a stronger compassionate connection with the earth itself.

> ### MINDFUL NATURE WALK
>
> Take in a few deep breaths as you start your walk. Take a moment to really notice the smell of the air, the temperature, the path ahead of you. Now, go for a "mindful walk"—walk silently, paying attention to your senses. With each walk you could pay particular attention to a particular sense—what you see (the colors, the textures, the shapes); what you hear; what you smell; what you feel (the temperature, your feet on the ground, the feel of the wind). When your mind wanders (as it inevitably will) to the past or the future rather than what you are currently experiencing, just notice that and bring yourself back to what you are hearing, smelling, seeing right in front of you. At the end of your walk, take three more deep breaths and again purposefully bring your attention to your surroundings and to how you feel. Try to embed those sensations in your brain. Then take a moment to journal. What did you learn about yourself or the world?

Interestingly, a number of students noted both how difficult it was to leave behind headphones and music/podcasts that they normally listened to while walking. Several stated that they had in the past struggled with a wandering mind, and that they had used music as a way to focus and relax while out walking. But without these buffers between them and their surroundings, and with specific instructions to pay close attention to their senses, they were amazed and awed at the beauty of the world. Their moods improved, and they felt calmer and more relaxed overall. They were surprised at their own capacity to see things, to focus and absorb the world around them. A number, in the words of Parker Palmer, found their "teacher within,"[12] drawing out lessons from nature—the natural rhythms of changing seasons, the adaptability and pliability of trees—and applying them to their lives.

While these initial mindful walks did not direct students toward making connections with the earth, a number of them did. They recognized at some level the ineffable sense of connection humans have with nature. One who was able to process a recent traumatic event commented on how "the forest seems to understand and respond" while another noted their growing awareness of the presence, if not sight, of the animals around them.

To build this connection further, I adapted a beholding exercise taught by economist Vaishali Mamgain at a teaching retreat organized by the Association for Contemplative Mind in Higher Education. For this assignment students were given the instruction to continue their mindful walks in nature, choosing a route they could return to each week and paying attention to their senses. This time, however, they were also to take note of any particular tree they were drawn to and then to spend five minutes beholding the tree—looking at it, "hanging out" with it, getting to know it. On the fourth and final visit students were to switch perspective and "see what the tree sees," or what it might be communicating.

TREE TIME

(15–20 MINUTES, ONCE A WEEK, FOR FOUR WEEKS)

Follow the instruction from the Mindful Nature Walk, but this time, make sure you choose a path you will be able to return to easily each week. During your mindful walk, notice if there is a particular tree that you are drawn to. Each week, spend at least five minutes simply gazing at the tree. Hang out with it. Get to know it. When something about the tree draws your attention—the colors, the patterns of the bark, whatever, *just keep looking*. Allow yourself to just look, like a kid watching a raindrop on a window or a cloud in the sky. Just be with the tree. You don't have to draw any conclusions; just keep looking. After each visit, note in your notebook what the experience was like for you.

> On your last visit to "your tree," after being with it for a few minutes, try to switch perspective and see what the tree sees. You can even ask the tree a question. Try to imagine what the tree would say, what it sees looking at you, what it is observing, what it might say to you, what it might be communicating.

According to Hart, practices such as beholding (rather than measuring or analyzing) can be helpful in developing a sense of connection to and concern for others by allowing in the emotional dimensions of experience.[13] Beholding allows the "other" to speak to us and creates a better understanding of others. Further, it allows for a sense of "attachment" to develop that can lead to "transformative understanding."[14] In choosing "their tree," as well as imagining its perspective, students were tapping into their other ways of knowing and connecting beyond speech and writing. As one expressed it, although the tree "could not talk in a language I could understand, he was able to communicate in other ways when I really decided to pay attention." The students were taking on a different, imagined perspective of an "other" and establishing a relationship with that (in this case, presumably inanimate) "other." In the words of another student:

> Switching my thinking and trying to look at things from the perspective of the tree was really interesting and kind of enjoyable to do. It was like trying to be empathetic towards something that isn't a person or animal and much more inanimate. It's odd because you can't tell or get really any clues from the tree itself to how it's feeling or what it's thinking about. But maybe that's the thing, is that it doesn't have anything to think about. It is just simply being.

And relationships did indeed develop. Trees were named, connected with as other living, feeling beings, became confidants, empathetic friends and teachers of profound life lessons (things change; one can bend but not break; leaning on others is normal). One wrote: "Weirdly, hugging this tree made me feel at home. [Trees] seem to realize that home is a place they build inside themselves rather than a place they find outside of themselves."

Students often felt deep empathy for the tree's possible experiences. One listed all the benefits trees provided, noted "how tired" they looked, and expressed her deep gratitude for all the work trees do to maintain life on Earth. They noticed, and felt for, broken limbs and lost neighbors. Thus, the students clearly did experience a profound sense of connection across the species barrier and they were learning to build on being present with themselves in order to connect with this "other." Further, they were learning that being connected and present does not necessarily require being physically together with another human being, speaking the same language. Connection was made when they tapped into their full range of senses and were open to receiving the world around them.

CONNECTING WITH OTHERS

Building on this sense of connection, some classes also engaged in loving-kindness practices that explicitly made the connection to other people with whom they did not have a personal connection. Such practices also seemed important in the context of the pandemic, where so little social connection was taking place, but also in the online environment in which many were living their social world. Ultimately this was a practice of presence (connection and compassion) with others even when those others were not necessarily physically "present." One class was asked to take the opportunity each day over two weeks to notice other people and silently wish them well—by touching in with a feeling of loving-kindness within themselves and sending that feeling out to the other. Once again students took up the challenge enthusiastically, enjoying the opportunity to be noticing and interacting with others. Many found the exercise comforting and good for their own well-being. One student noted:

I WISH YOU WELL

For the next two weeks, at least once a day when you're out of the house, walking or driving to or from a destination, try to notice the individuals around you and silently wish them well. This could be people walking by you on the street, or other drivers (this is best at stoplights when there's a driver you can see also waiting for the light to turn). Make a practice to notice them (you're not making eye contact, although if you do, you can always smile and nod, but this is just an internal noticing and sending good wishes). Bring your attention to the other person and mentally send them a wish for health, happiness, ease—whatever works for you. You can say to yourself "May you [other person I don't know] be healthy, may you be happy, may you be at ease," or "May your day go okay," or "May something good happen to you today," or some phrase that works for you. Try to bring your full but very momentary attention to the other person and send a sense of warmth or care toward them. You can draw on that warmth you feel when you think of someone you care about (or your pet, or a bag of chips . . .). Try to do this at least once a day for the next couple of weeks (or at least ten times over the next two weeks). Make it a habit of what you do when you're walking or driving somewhere. Play with it. Then write up a one-page journal entry on what it was like, what you experienced, what you observed.

> The "well wishes and good vibes" assignment, as I have so affectionately dubbed this latest journal entry, seemed interesting to me from the very outset. I like to think of myself as a very caring person, especially towards those in my "bubble." Disconnecting that sense of caring from my core group friends and family and extending it to strangers, even in this small way, I admit . . . is something I really hadn't thought to do. . . . All in all, I found this exercise to be very enjoyable and even cathartic. Wishing others well and honestly hoping that good things happen for them helps me feel more connected to people in an intensely disconnected time.

Some students noticed that their curiosity about other people was piqued, as was their sense of solidarity and mutuality ("They're just like me"). One remarked that they found the process "comforting," changing their outlook on others and the world as a whole for the better: "Looking at others and having warm thoughts and wishing them well as they pass by whilst going about their days, it makes me wonder if people have ever looked at me and wished me well when I am the one passing by on the street or in a shop. The world really could use a reminder of an optimistic outlook on things, especially in the current state of disarray the globe is in at the present moment."

Another mused:

> Wishing people well over this past number of weeks has gotten me to notice that even the smallest gestures can make a big difference in people's lives. Just wishing someone well and [sending] good vibes . . . makes me feel happy, and makes me feel that maybe I had an impact on someone's life. . . . *The people who I wished well did not notice me, but I noticed them.* I noticed if they looked tired or stressed, what they were doing at the moment; and it made me wonder how people are feeling and coping with emotions and thoughts during this tough and unprecedented time.

That is, the exercise helped students to connect with others who—like icons on a screen—are not necessarily engaged or connected in return. Rather, the sense of connection relies on the students' inner presence to their own feelings of well-being and sending that out to others.

One of the major complaints about online classes that we have heard in the aftermath of the era of emergency remote learning is that students felt no sense of connection and therefore no sense of "draw" or responsibility toward the class and their classmates. Using this exercise during an online class provided a way of at least beginning to build that connection to each other. Even with cameras off, they focused on an icon or a name of someone else in the class and wished them well, just as they had with strangers. Ultimately, the exercise showed students that they can actively create and strengthen connection and compassion, even in the online space, despite seeming barriers of space and technology.

CONNECTING OUTSIDE AND INSIDE THE ONLINE CLASSROOM

The experience of reading my students' journals also helped me overcome the difficulties of connecting with them as real humans in the online class. In the virtual class, few turned on their cameras or engaged in discussion. But online learning doesn't only take place in the synchronous classroom, as Palalas (this volume) points out. The asynchronous engagement with content can create another space for meaningful interaction and the development of presence. Their journal reflections let me understand them as people rather than icons on a screen. Perhaps the most productive outcome of these journals was how they invited *me* into students' inner worlds. I did not have to be physically with them in the classroom; I was able to be truly present with them as they walked the world, and to bear witness to their moments of self-awareness and birthing of profound insights and reflections. Reading and responding to their journal entries allowed me to be present with them in the online asynchronous space of the learning platform—often my only one-on-one interaction with them. And indeed, by remaining fully present in this interaction, I felt connected to my students in a way I had rarely managed in the past, even during in-person classes.

I had, in the past, always been careful to maintain the line of professional separation from students, but the journals required no judgment of their abilities (they received full marks just for doing the journal), only a human-to-human response. I would often find myself relating to their experiences and commenting "Isn't that amazing how . . . ?" (even "I love how") based on my own similar experiences and reflections. While not all of them read the feedback (the beauty of the online marking system is that I knew when they did), the impact on me and my own orientation toward the students was palpable. I no longer viewed them as resistant and unknowable, as mere icons on a screen, but as fellow human beings with whom I had shared some profound moments and insights. I could remember and re-create that somatic sense of fellow feeling when I saw their names: "Oh yes, this is the one who saw the tree as a grandmother / had the bravery to actually talk out loud to the tree / talked about their childhood memories of the smell of leaves," just like I have.

This kind of interaction, however, required me to be truly present, even in this asynchronous, online space, to the students, as whole beings. Indeed, perhaps because the online space made it painfully clear that what I was trying to teach my students—that connection is a matter of effort, not an automatic product of proximity—was also true for me as a teacher. I couldn't rely on trying to be funny or nice in the classroom as a stand-in for connection. Marking their journals was one of the few spaces available to make that connection, and it required me to make a real effort, to put myself in an open and self-aware space—not pushing down my emotional/somatic reactions or "nonrational" responses.

The journals were full of insights that showed students were being vulnerable and sharing personal insights that were profound and precious for them. Responding in kind required deep listening and great care so that this trust would not be betrayed. This kind of engaged marking required even more effort and focus than more traditional intellectual grading, and spoke to the need for "less" and "slower" in terms of assignments. It was admittedly a struggle in such a difficult year to keep up this level of openness and presence, and I could often feel myself slipping back into more rote responses; but with each assignment, I did try to make at least one real connection that came from the heart, not the head. In this way we were able to build an open and trusting space in the asynchronous online space (see Palalas, this volume; Wong, this volume).

The intimacy of this connection was most clear in the nature-based exercises, where the students' journal entries about the visceral experience of being in nature, walking mindfully or beholding a tree, allowed me to be there with them and witness them developing insights into themselves and the world around them. It was a delightful connection as I experienced their world (including students who were conducting their mindful walks in far-flung places) and could in some ways be with them as they reflected and processed. I was able to be part of their world for a short while in a way even office-hour or post-class chats would not allow me to be. And in those moments, I felt truly present with them—not as teacher to student, but as humans on the planet. I wasn't physically with them, but we were experiencing these moments together—even if asynchronously. We were truly present "in and with" the content of their journals (Palalas, this volume).

These moments also echo what Shari Geller refers to as "relational presence": an "intersubjective state of consciousness" in which we "feel a sense of resonance with [an other's] experience as if it were our own, allowing us to see, feel and experience aspects of their inner world that we would not otherwise have access to."[15] We can then listen to our attuned bodily resonance, which evokes responses that are intuitive and directly emerging from [the other's] unspoken experience. It evokes a flow of energy that is healing in and of itself."[16] This kind of connection to each other perhaps opened the possibilities of the classroom—which has always been so much bigger than a physical space, and always in some ways at a distance—as a healing space.

Thus, these contemplative exercises may have laid the groundwork for building a more just society, introducing us to this healing flow of energy that is required for transformative personal and social change, around, within, and through the online space. Both my students and I learned to be more present to ourselves. And being more present to our full selves allowed us to grow our capacity to be more compassionately connected to each other, and the world around us, both offline and online.

NOTES

1. Research Ethics UNB REB#044-2018.
2. Interestingly, Buber (1958) describes "a spiritual electricity that surges between people when they relate authentically and humanly"—part of what Geller refers to as "relational presence." Shari M. Geller, *A Practical Guide to Cultivating Relational Presence* (The American Psychological Association, 2017).
3. bell hooks, *Teaching to Transgress: Education as the Practice of Freedom* (New York: Routledge, 1994).
4. This interconnection is slowly being acknowledged in studies of social change. See, for example, Christine Wamsler et al., "Linking Internal and External Transformation for Sustainability and Climate Action: Towards a New Research and Policy Agenda," *Global Environmental Change* 71 (November 2021).
5. Heesoon Bai, Charles Scott, and Beatrice Donald, "Contemplative Pedagogy and the Revitalization of Teacher Education," *Alberta Journal of Educational Research* 55, no. 3 (2005): 320–21.
6. Ronald Purser, *McMindfulness: How Mindfulness Became the New Capitalist Spirituality* (United Kingdom: Watkins Media, 2019). See, also, David Forbes, *Mindfulness and Its Discontents: Education, Self, and Social Transformation* (Halifax, Nova Scotia: Fernwood Publishing, 2019).
7. Christopher Gemer and Kristin Neff, *The Mindfulness Self-Compassion Workbook* (New York: Guilford Press, 2018), 9–14.
8. David Kahane, "Learning about Obligation, Compassion and Global Justice: The Place of Contemplative Pedagogy," *New Directions for Teaching and Learning* 118 (2009): 52.
9. David A. Treleaven, *Trauma-Sensitive Mindfulness: Practices for Safe and Transformative Healing* (New York: W. W. Norton, 2018).
10. Kristin Neff, "Self-Compassion: An Alternative Conceptualization of a Healthy Attitude toward Oneself," *Self and Identity* 2 (2003): 85–102.
11. This is in line with much of the literature on the beneficial effects of nature on well-being. See Colin Capaldi et al., "Flourishing in Nature: A Review of the Benefits of Connecting with Nature and Its Application as a Wellbeing Intervention," *International Journal of Wellbeing* 5, no. 4 (2015): 1–16, doi:10.5502/ijw.v5i4.
12. Parker Palmer, *The Courage to Teach* (San Francisco: Jossey-Bass, 2017).
13. Tobin Hart, "Opening the Contemplative Mind in the Classroom," *Journal of Transformative Education* 2, no. 1 (January 2004): 33.
14. Hart, "Opening the Contemplative Mind," 33.
15. Geller, *A Practical Guide*, 200.
16. Ibid.

BIBLIOGRAPHY

Bai, Heesoon, Charles Scott and Beatrice Donald. "Contemplative Pedagogy and the Revitalization of Teacher Education." *Alberta Journal of Educational Research* 55, no. 3 (Fall 2009): 319–34.

Berila, Beth. *Integrating Mindfulness into Anti-Oppression Pedagogy: Social Justice in Higher Education*. New York: Routledge, 2016.

Capaldi, Colin A., Holly-Ann Passmore, Elizabeth K, Nisbet, John M. Zelenski, and Raelyne L. Dopko. "Flourishing in Nature: A Review of the Benefits of Connecting with Nature and Its Application as a Wellbeing Intervention." *International Journal of Wellbeing* 5, no. 4 (2015): 1–16. doi:10.5502/ijw.v5i4.1

Doran, Peter. *A Political Economy of Attention, Mindfulness and Consumerism: Reclaiming the Mindful Commons*. New York: Routledge, 2017.

Hart, Tobin. "Opening the Contemplative Mind in the Classroom." *Journal of Transformative Education* 2, no. 1 (January 2004): 28–46.

hooks, bell. *Teaching to Transgress: Education as the Practice of Freedom*. New York: Routledge, 1994.

Forbes, David. "Critical Integral Contemplative Education." In *Handbook of Mindfulness: Culture, Context and Social Engagement*, edited by Ronald E. Purser, David Forbes, and Adam Burke, 355–67. New York: Springer, 2016.

Forbes, David. *Mindfulness and Its Discontents: Education, Self, and Social Transformation*. Halifax, Nova Scotia: Fernwood Publishing, 2019.

Geller, Shari M. *A Practical Guide to Cultivating Relational Presence*. The American Psychological Association, 2017. http://dx.doi.org/10.1037/0000025-012.

Gemer, Christopher, and Kristin Neff. *The Mindfulness Self-Compassion Workbook*. New York, Guilford Press, 2018. ["Self-compassion Guided Practices and Exercises. Exercise 1: How would you treat a friend?" https://self-compassion.org/exercise-1-treat-friend/]

Kahane, David. "Learning about Obligation, Compassion and Global Justice: The Place of Contemplative Pedagogy." *New Directions for Teaching and Learning* 118 (2009).

Neff, Kristin. "Self-Compassion: An Alternative Conceptualization of a Healthy Attitude toward Oneself." *Self and Identity* 2 (2003): 85–102.

Palmer, Parker. *The Courage to Teach: Exploring the Inner Landscape of a Teacher's Life*. 20th Anniversary Edition. San Francisco, CA: Jossey-Bass, 2017.

Purser, Ronald. *McMindfulness: How Mindfulness Became the New Capitalist Spirituality*. United Kingdom: Watkins Media, 2019.

Treleaven, David A. *Trauma-Sensitive Mindfulness: Practices for Safe and Transformative Healing*. New York: W. W. Norton, 2018.

Wamsler, Christine, Gustav Osberg, Walter Osika, Heidi Herndersson, and Luis Mundaca. "Linking Internal and External Transformation for Sustainability and Climate Action: Towards a New Research and Policy Agenda." *Global Environmental Change* 71 (November 2021): Article 102373. https://doi.org/10.1016/j.gloenvcha.2021.102373.

Wapner, Paul. "Contemplative Environmental Studies: Pedagogy for Self and Planet," *The Journal of Contemplative Inquiry* 3, no. 1 (2016): 67–83.

Chapter Eight

Guided Practice 2

Presence with/in/of Nature: Sit Spot Practice and Forest Therapy Walks

Monika Stelzl

I invite you to put this reading down, wander about, and find a comfortable spot. I suggest a spot by a window, outside, or near some nature being, such as a plant or an animal companion. For the next ten to fifteen minutes (set a timer if you need to), just sit, lie down, or wander around slowly if that is what is calling you. With nowhere else to be and nothing else to do.

Welcome back. Before you continue reading, take a few moments to reflect on what you are noticing.

This activity is often called *the sit spot practice* and it involves being quietly in a spot in nature for a period of time, usually about fifteen to twenty minutes. I incorporate this practice in a third-year undergraduate experiential psychology course called The Psychology of Human-Nature Connection. The course is taught over the period of a fall term (the length of which is approximately twelve to thirteen weeks). That way, students can be outdoors as much as possible while engaging with this practice, given that we live in Atlantic Canada with a colder winter climate.

Across the semester, students are asked to practice the sit spot weekly for a period of ten weeks. I encourage them to have one or two regular outdoor sit spots, but also to be flexible in terms of weather, energy/self-care, and so on. Once the weather gets cooler, the sit spot is moved inside, ideally near a window. Students are asked to share a post once a week in an online discussion forum. They can reflect on their sit spot practice with words such as poetry, pictures, and anything else that speaks to them during that week.

Another experiential component incorporated in the course consists of forest therapy walks. In the Western context (e.g., North America), the practice of forest therapy walks reflects a guided sensory immersion journey. Forest therapy, as we know it in the West, has been to some degree inspired by the Japanese practice of shinrin-yoku, also known as forest bathing (and that term is sometimes used in the West as well). Shinrin-yoku means "taking in the forest atmosphere, or forest bathing"[1] by drawing on our senses, such as sounds and touch, to experience relaxation and a decrease in stress.[2]

In a similar vein to forest bathing, the role of a forest therapy guide is to facilitate participants' own connection with the forest or the natural environment. One of the mottos or sayings used is "The forest is the therapist. The guide opens the doors."[3] To develop the course and incorporate forest therapy or forest bathing as a part of student experiential learning, I undertook specialized training to become a certified forest therapy guide. I trained with the Association of Nature and Forest Therapy Guides and Programs (ANFT) in 2019, and pursued additional training with Global Institute of Forest Therapy (GIFT) in 2021.

As a guide, I am trained to create a space where people can slow down and hence notice more readily their immediate (i.e., in the here and now) sensory experiences. Other key aspects of a forest therapy walk include the focus on a reciprocal relationship with nature and on pleasurable sensory experiences. A forest therapy walk is usually done in person, but during the COVID-19 pandemic, it was adapted by some guides to also being offered remotely (e.g., via Zoom).

In the experiential course, I guide students on three to four forest therapy walks. In one version of the course, when all courses were taught remotely due to the pandemic, all the walks were led remotely. In another rendering of the course, in the fall of 2021, we had two walks in person and two walks were led remotely. Given the circumstances of the pandemic in relation to online teaching and learning, I adapted the remotely led walks in a way that provided students with the option of being either inside or outside. Therefore, if students were not able to be in a forest or a park due to a local pandemic lockdown, a lack of mobile data, or barriers associated with access to natural spaces, they were still able to experience a sensory connection with nature in some way.

Remotely guided walks were facilitated via Zoom with students being encouraged to use either a cell phone or a tablet with earbuds or headphones rather than a computer or a laptop to allow for the movement of one's body. To further facilitate sensory connection with their surroundings, students were asked to keep one earbud off their ear to be able to notice sounds in the place they were in, and to turn off notifications to limit distractions. Students who were inside for the duration of the remotely guided walk were encouraged to be by a window and have a nature-being or a part of nature nearby, such as a plant or a rock, a piece of fruit or vegetable, or even a glass of water. Together as a class, we developed a list of quiet spaces on campus and around our smaller city where Wi-Fi was available, so the students who were not able to have a quiet space at home or at school were aware of the location of quieter environments.

Each walk was about two to two and a half hours in length. If done outside, we did not go very far, and I highlighted the sensory aspects of being in nature. When led remotely with the likelihood of some students being inside, the possibility of exploring natural features of their surroundings was offered. Regardless of the format of the walk (in person or remotely guided), the emphasis was on a very slow pace so as to allocate time for students to slow down, awaken their senses, and connect with the forest/natural aspects of their environment via a series of sensory invitations. One such sensory invitation is included at the end of this chapter.

In the class following a guided walk, we collectively shared the experience. When debriefing about the remotely led walks afterward, several students noted that their transition from the nature-exploration practice back to "regular" life was somewhat abrupt, and for some, jarring. Thus, we collectively developed a set of suggestions of what activity (or nonactivity) a person could consider after the completion of the guided walk in order to enhance their integration with the nature sensory-immersion experience. Some ideas were taking a slow walk (especially if the practice was done inside), taking a (short) rest or a bath, or engaging in a mindful preparation and eating of a meal without other distractions.

Furthermore, after each walk/sensory-immersion practice, students were required to make two posts in an online discussion forum dedicated to each walk. They had one week to complete these posts so as to provide time for integration and reflection on the practice. For each walk, students also submitted a longer written reflection on anything related to their forest therapy walk experience. My aim with this reflexive assignment was for students to be present as much as possible during the walks without needing to think about the assignment itself (i.e., to move away from goal-oriented learning). To minimize the evaluative aspect that can be associated with academic assignments, the marking of the reflections was either a full mark for submission and meeting the length criterion (500 to 750 words per reflection) or zero for non-submission. To further encourage an agenda-free experience, I provided students with the following guidelines for the assignment in the course's syllabus:

> The aim of these assignments is to take time to reflect on each of the walks. Among other possibilities, reflective writing gives us a way to consider our experiences, observations, and shifts in feelings, thoughts, beliefs, and so on. The reflection note can contain a description of the experience, but it should also contain a reflection on that experience so your own understanding of the experiential learning grows in this reflective process. Given that the walks themselves *do not* have a set agenda (such as to have a profound experience), the reflection notes can be about anything related to the walks. You can reflect on your thoughts and feelings prior to the first walk (esp. if you have never been on

a forest therapy walk before), and for the subsequent walks, as well—what have you felt after a walk, what are you noticing when in nature after a walk, and so on. Ideally, I would like you to just be present during the walks without thinking about what to write in the reflection note. It may take some practice to "be a participant" during a forest therapy walk rather than a student. Similarly, I will be practicing being a forest therapy guide during our walks rather than a professor. You can explore this "balancing act" or process in your reflection notes. The aim is for you to take time to reflect on the walks and your own experience *after* the walks are conducted rather than during a walk.

One of my primary aspirations in the nature-based experiential course is to facilitate students' connection or reconnection with nature and their own sensory landscape. As of the time of writing this vignette (spring 2022), I have taught the course three times. Across those three instances, the major takeaway from the course that was repeatedly articulated by students has been one of connection. Noticeable shifts happen in how the nature-oriented focus of the course is perceived, with a sense of connection unfolding and deepening throughout the term.

For example, at the beginning of the term, students tend to express that having a nature-based experiential course is quite different from their other courses. Invariably, across the three offerings of the course, students initially noted that they felt that the sit spot practice was taking them away from homework from other courses (I did remind them that the sit spot practice was also a type of homework). Their perception changed over the course of the term, with students increasingly expressing a deeper connection with nature and each other, as well as articulating increased presence in their bodies along with a sense of gratitude for these practices during the atypical and challenging terms of the COVID-19 pandemic.

While becoming a certified forest therapy guide involves several months of training and financial cost, I think one does not have to be a forest therapy guide in order to incorporate nature-based experiential practices in their course(s). The sit spot practice can be done as an ongoing assignment or as a stand-alone invitation at the start of class (outside or inside), and a simple sensory-based invitation to notice nature can be developed without specialized training.

In that spirit, I offer a simple invitation that, like the sit spot, can provide a sensory-based opening to any class:

Sensory Invitation
(approximately 15 minutes; outside or inside)
Explore the place you are in with your sense of touch or your sense of hearing. Feel free to have your eyes closed, or open. If you feel you've completed exploring with one sense, feel free to switch your exploration to the other sense. After the invitation, take a few moments to reflect on what you are noticing.

NOTES

1. Yuko Tsunetsugu, Bum-Jin Park, and Yoshifumi Miyazaki, "Trends in Research Related to 'Shinrin-Yoku' (Taking in the Forest Atmosphere or Forest Bathing) in Japan," *Environmental Health and Preventive Medicine* 15, no. 1 (July 9, 2009): 27–37, doi:10.1007/s12199-009-0091-z.

2. Margaret M. Hansen, Reo Jones, and Kirsten Tocchini, "Shinrin-Yoku (Forest Bathing) and Nature Therapy: A State-of-the-Art Review." *International Journal of Environmental Research and Public Health* 14, no.8 (2017): 851, doi:10.3390/ijerph14080851.

3. Ben Page and M. Amos Clifford, "A Guide's Handbook of Forest Therapy, Module 1, 2020," https://anft.thinkific.com/courses/take/anft-member-resources/pdfs/20770953-guides-handbook-of-forest-therapy-introduction.

BIBLIOGRAPHY

Hansen MM, Jones R, Tocchini K. "Shinrin-Yoku (Forest Bathing) and Nature Therapy: A State-of-the-Art Review." *International Journal of Environmental Research and Public Health* 14, no.8 (2017): 851, doi:10.3390/ijerph14080851.

Page, Ben, and M. Amos Clifford. "A Guide's Handbook of Forest Therapy," Module 1, 2020. https://anft.thinkific.com/courses/take/anft-member-resources/pdfs/20770953-guides-handbook-of-forest-therapy-introduction.

Tsunetsugu, Yuko, Bum-Jin Park, and Yoshifumi Miyazaki. "Trends in Research Related to 'Shinrin-Yoku' (Taking in the Forest Atmosphere or Forest Bathing) in Japan." *Environmental Health and Preventive Medicine* 15, no. 1 (July 9, 2009): 27–37. doi:10.1007/s12199-009-0091-z.

Chapter Nine

Fresh Eyes, Beginner's Mind
Contemplative Photography and a Walking-Based Pedagogy of Embodied Presence When the World Goes Online

Yuk-Lin Renita Wong

As I reflect on what to write about online presence in this chapter, my mind keeps returning to what the students shared in the last class in a graduate course I taught in the past two years during the global COVID-19 pandemic. Toward the end of this last class, students were asked to share their takeaway from the course and to express their appreciation to each other for their co-learning journey. One student thanked their peers for bringing vulnerability to the space that also allowed them to be vulnerable. Upon this student's comment, more students shared similar experiences of feeling that it was safe to be vulnerable in the course. One student said people could "actually see each other in the eye" despite meeting remotely on Zoom. There was a sense of "genuine and personal connection." It was an "intimate space" where students were present with each other.

This overall sense of a safe space for vulnerability in the course from the previous year was echoed during this past year. A student shared that they felt brave to express themselves in this course. This was "a big deal" to them, as they mostly stayed quiet in other courses. One student felt more of themselves, "more of Life," and said the course provided a space where all experiences—vulnerability, struggle, laughter, goofiness—were welcomed. Another student felt comfortable with being herself and connecting with others in the course, which helped her slowly reclaim her body that was rejected in the dominant discourse of the society. These students were racialized, gender-nonconforming, neurodiverse, and/or of marginalized religious backgrounds.

The students' comments about the course being a safe space for vulnerability came to me as a pleasant surprise, especially given the largely remote class space. Although I was intentional in making major adjustments to this graduate course to support and engage students in remote learning during the pandemic, I would not have imagined that a remote class space could be a safe space for vulnerability. The students' feedback prompted me to look back more closely at what I did in the course, pedagogically, that held this safe and welcoming space in supporting students' presence with each other in a largely remote learning environment.

In the following, I will briefly describe the course and its intentions, followed by a discussion of the walking-based pedagogy used in this course to cultivate students' open and receptive embodied presence to themselves, to their physical and social environment, and to each other. I will introduce the Mindful Walking Project, which formed the major course assignment, with a particular focus on the students' experience of the Miksang photography exercise. I will then discuss how the creation of a co-learning community through weekly check-in sharing further supported students' sense of connectedness. I hope to show that online presence is less about what we do with the technology and more about how we engage students in embodied practices that enhance their capacity to stay grounded and present, online or offline, as well as how we create a co-learning space for collective presence.

THE COURSE: MINDFULNESS AND JUST RELATIONS IN SOCIAL WORK

This graduate course introduced students to mindfulness (*sati*) as a political act and embodied ethics in social justice and critical social work. Mindfulness in Pali is *sati* (Sanskrit: *smṛti*), which means remembering, recollecting, bearing in mind. It involves remembering to come back to the present moment.[1] Mindfulness is open and spacious embodied awareness of what is present in this moment. It supports a nonreactive observation of what is happening just as it is, internally and externally; and it is an inquiry into the "habits of mind": the "habitual" and taken-for-granted thinking, feeling, and acting in the personal and systemic realms, and in the social and natural world. As a contemplative practice rooted in Buddhist onto-epistemology, mindfulness is a radical act that begins with the "self" and yet illuminates the "illusion of self," i.e., the illusion of "self" as an unchanging, separate, and independent entity or existence. As an embodied practice, mindfulness brings forth an embodied awareness of "self" as process, as relations, as "interbeing." Looking deeply into life and all existence, Thich Nhat Hanh observed: "To be is to inter-be."[2] As such, mindfulness calls for one's ethical engagement in the social and natural world as we make the world and are made of it.

The course was intended for students to: 1) gain hands-on mindfulness practice, based on the classic text, *The Four Establishments of Mindfulness* (*Satipaṭṭhāna Sutta*); 2) refine their sensory awareness, observation, and inquiry into internal and external phenomena and environment; 3) practice the teaching that "social justice is every step" in the relational ethics of "self" with others and the world, place, and the Earth, human and nonhuman, animate and inanimate; and 4) apply mindfulness in critical social work practice.

As in most mindfulness courses, students learned basic mindfulness practices such as mindful breathing, walking, and eating. When this course was offered in person before the pandemic, students were asked to practice either sitting meditation or a body scan[3] of thirty minutes daily, five days a week. During the summer of 2020 when I prepared to teach this course in a blended format in the fall, with two-thirds synchronous remote sessions and one-third in-person sessions, I was aware of the Zoom fatigue many were experiencing from sitting in front of the computer screen for hours. I knew it would be more beneficial for students to learn trauma-informed mindfulness practices outdoors that would support them to reconnect with themselves and their environment (social and physical), considering the possible exacerbation of mental health issues some students might be facing as a result of the anxiety over COVID-19 infection and social isolation from lockdown and social distancing. I decided to experiment with a "walking-based pedagogy"[4] to incorporate more outdoor and movement-based mindfulness practices, in hopes of helping students tune in to their bodies, their physical environments, and the Earth through their five senses. Instead of sitting meditation or body scan, mindful walking was therefore adopted as the main practice in the course.

A WALKING-BASED PEDAGOGY OF EMBODIED PRESENCE

Mindful Walking

Mindful walking is a meditative practice in motion. Students were asked to gently bring their attention to the sensations of contact between their feet and the ground, and to feel the motion of their body as they walked. They were also invited to coordinate their breathing with their steps. As instructed by Thich Nhat Hanh in his dharma talks, "Breathing in, I take one step. Breathing out, I take another step." Or, students could say silently as they took one step, "Arriving"; and "Here and Now" as they took the next step. In walking meditation, we are not walking to go somewhere, or anywhere. I told the students that the address of their destination was "here and now." We are arriving in the here and the now with each step. Most often, when we walk, we walk with projects in our head, with anxiety or worries about the future, or regrets about the past. Mindful walking brings us back to the present moment with each step as we walk. It helps the mind come back to the body, to quiet down and to gain clarity about what is here.

Before the pandemic, I had always introduced mindful walking as an important mindfulness practice in motion that students would incorporate into their daily life. In preparing for the remote teaching of this course, however, I was inspired by Feinberg's inquiry into the pedagogical potential of walking[5] and the Mindful Walking Project, which was a participatory action research project "to advance the theory and practice of walking and sensory research methodologies."[6] I was interested in experimenting with how Miksang photography,[7] tree contemplation,[8] and soundscape[9] could be integrated into mindful walking to enhance students' sensory awareness of and engagement with their environment (social, ecological, and political).

In *The Four Establishments of Mindfulness* (*Satipaṭṭhāna Sutta*), mindfulness of the body in the body is the first establishment of mindfulness. The English translation, "mindfulness," can be misleading, as it seems to focus exclusively on the mind. In fact, we can be present only when we are grounded in the body. The body anchors us in the present, while the mind often takes us into the past or the future. When the mind is not present, we are more likely to go on autopilot with our conditionings and get driven by the "background feelings" of liking or disliking. Observing these underlying feeling tones (Pali: *vedanā*)—pleasant, unpleasant, and neutral—is the second establishment of mindfulness. When the mind is connected to the body in the present, we are less swept away by our habitual thinking and feeling that colors our perceptions. "Being present," Lata Mani wrote in a contemplative essay, "means cultivating a deep cognizance of one's mental habits, emotional tendencies and preferences" as she witnessed, grieved, and honored her experiences through her recovery journey from a serious brain injury.[10] Mindfulness creates a pause between our conditionings and what is happening in the present. It makes it more possible for us to catch our conditioned reactivity and discern appropriate action in response to what is being experienced in the present.

Our body meets the world through the senses of sight, hearing, smell, taste, and touch. When we are grounded in sensory awareness, we have a brief moment, however fleeting, to meet and *know* the world before the conceptual mind jumps in to categorize and filter what we see, hear, smell, taste, or touch based on our past conditioning and preferences. Bhante Gunaratana identifies this preconceptual awareness as "bare attention":

> When you first become aware of something, there is a fleeting instant of pure awareness just before you conceptualize the thing, before you identify it. That is a state of awareness. Ordinarily, this state is short-lived. It is that flashing split second just as you focus your eyes on the thing, just as you focus your mind on the thing, just before you objectify it, clamp down on it mentally, and segregate it from the rest of existence. It takes place just before you start thinking about it—before your mind says, "Oh, it's a dog."[11]

I would further argue that when we are able to tune in to this transient moment, we are more likely to meet and know the world with a beginner's mind. As Zen teacher Suzuki Roshi wrote, "In the beginner's mind there are many possibilities, but in the expert's there are few."[12] A beginner's mind is not yet filled with concepts, opinions, and judgments. It is not yet bound by the ego. This allows for an opening to a spacious and receptive presence to the in-between space of self and other where novel ideas and approaches, and new ways of relating to others and the world, can emerge.[13]

The Mindful Walking Project

The major assignment in the Mindfulness and Just Relations in Social Work course was a Mindful Walking Project. Students learned and incorporated the practices of contemplative Miksang photography, tree contemplation, and listening to the soundscape of their environment into their daily mindful walking practice. Within the limits of this chapter, I will focus on the students' experience of the contemplative Miksang photography exercise (which I will explain later) in the Mindful Walking Project.

The Mindful Walking Project was place-based, relational, and material. Building on the importance of sensory inquiry and embodiment in place and the Earth, it was intended to support students to cultivate embodied awareness and establish relationships with themselves, and their lived social, natural, and built environment in their neighborhood. The project comprised three components:

1. Freewriting: In the first week of the course, students were asked to do a freewriting of no more than ten minutes on what they knew about their neighborhood, where they most often visited or passed by, or what stood out to them in their neighborhood. The freewriting was not graded but would be a reference point for them to return to later when they wrote their final paper.
2. Photo essay: Building on the contemplative Miksang photography exercises, students took images of their neighborhood and reflected on what they had learned from noticing the "ordinary" in their daily lived environment; what habits (their preferences, thinking or behavioral patterns, biases, assumptions, or social conditionings) they had noticed in how they related to their lived environment, social, natural, and built; where these habits came from or how they had been formed; in what ways these habits were beneficial, or not, to them, others, and their lived environment; and what they would like to do about these habits as they became aware of them.

3. Final paper: Students were asked to reflect on the entire embodied process and sensory awareness and inquiry of their neighborhood in the Mindful Walking Project based on the photos they took, the neighborhood soundscape they mapped, their daily mindful walking practice logs, weekly reflective reading journals, and class discussion. With reference to the embodied epistemology and ethical foundations of mindfulness, students were asked to reflect on what they had learned about their neighborhood that they did not know at the time when they freewrote about their neighborhood, their relationship and responsibility to their lived environment (social, natural, and built), and in what ways their learning and experience in the Mindful Walking Project informed their critical social work practice for social justice.

The focus on students' place-based embodiment of knowing through their sensory awareness was a decolonial pedagogical move. In social work programs—including mine—that center critical or anti-oppressive social work education, students are taught structural and poststructuralist analysis and critical reflexivity, which mostly privileges conceptual-analytical thinking in deconstructing power. Though other forms of knowing and transformation through the body, affect, and spirit have slowly been recognized in recent years with the recognition of Indigenous and non-Euro-Western worldviews and knowledge systems, their contribution to social work practice has been little understood, or, worse still, resisted. As Mensinga and Pyles emphatically argue in their introduction to a special issue of the journal *Australian Social Work* dedicated to embodiment and social work,

> a focus on exploring embodiment is especially salient in this moment amid innumerable social injustices, climate crisis, and a global pandemic. In the context of digital global capitalism, many of us find ourselves spending too many of our waking hours sitting and clicking in front of screens, disconnecting us from the felt sense of ourselves including basic somatic cues such as thirst, muscular tension, and fatigue.[14]

For social workers facing mounting community needs—material, psychological, socioeconomic—as well as budget cuts and burnout from high-pressure environments, attending to embodiment is not only timely but long overdue. In this course, the Mindful Walking Project was not only intended to reconnect students to the materiality of their body in relation to their physical environment, the Earth, and the interbeing of all lives, but also for non-Indigenous students to reflect on our ethical engagement with the Indigenous peoples of this land.

Miksang Photography and Receptive Presence

Miksang is a Tibetan word that translates as "good eye." Miksang contemplative photography brings together the art of photography, the discipline of meditation, and the Dharma Art teachings of Chögyam Trungpa.[15] It is said that we all have a "good eye" as part of our human makeup. This means we have the ability to see the world in a "pure way," without overlays of concepts, like, or dislike.[16] This is the quality of mindfulness.

As a form of contemplative photography, Miksang asks us to see the world with fresh eyes. When we can see with our "good eye," the world is always fresh, because everything we see is as if for the first time. There are no associations or preconceptions, only the world manifesting to us, as it is, vivid and alive. If we can place our awareness in our preconceptual sense of sight, we can connect with what we see, directly and intimately. This requires quieting the mind and the desire to really see what is there so that we can express what we are seeing with the camera simply and spontaneously, free from the normative expectation and framing of beauty.

Students in this course were introduced to mindful walking in the second week of an in-person class outdoors. For five days in the following week, students practiced ten minutes of a very slow mindful walk and twenty minutes of a mindful walk at their usual pace, and journaled their observations and experiences daily. The mindful walking practice set the foundation for students to stay grounded in their steps when Miksang photography was incorporated into their daily mindful walk in the third week. Students first learned a very simple "Flash of Color" exercise which combined the "Flash of Perception" and "Color as Color" exercises in introductory Miksang photography. They closed their eyes or kept a soft gaze downcast and slowly spun around so that they did not know their exact orientation. They then paused, opened their eyes, and noticed the first sight of color, which a student later called "a pop of color." It did not matter what they saw. They just stayed with what caught their eye before labeling it or before they could even tell what it was. This is the moment of preconceptual awareness Bhante Gunaratana describes. Students then filled the camera viewfinder or screen with the specific and unique elements of what they saw in that flash of color. This usually meant that they needed to walk over to where the pop of color appeared and then fill the viewfinder or screen with the specific sighting that had drawn their attention.

This exercise appears simple, but it was mind-blowing for many students. One student was delighted to "discover" a bench painted with rainbow colors on the street near their house during their first mindful walk, doing the Flash of Color exercise. They had lived in this neighborhood for several years but had never noticed this rainbow bench! Another student caught a white speck on a field of green. When they went over to take a picture, their mind was quick to label this white speck as a piece of garbage on the ground. It brought an abrupt shift in their attitude and judgment of something which was initially just a white speck on a field of green in the moment of sensory awareness. It was a pivotal experience for this student to realize what labeling did—not in an intellectual way, but as an embodied experience through their sight sensory awareness. This experience prompted them to become more intentional in meeting others and the world with more open receptivity. They were more willing to pause and hold space for things and people they were initially quick to judge and push away, and to *see* the multifaceted nature of characters and phenomena. Students in my program learn about discourse and power. The Flash of Color exercise sensitized their cognizance and deconstruction of discourses and power not just intellectually, but through their embodied sight sense that would percolate into their consciousness.

In the "Way of Light"[17] Miksang photography exercise, students were initially asked to just notice light and work with light as light. They started with the first assignment of taking pictures of patches of light or patches of shadow, such as a patch of light on the floor, or a pattern of shadow created by leaves or other objects on the wall. Very simple. Very ordinary. Patches of light or shadow can be in the form of stripes or bars or dots and so forth. The point is to keep it simple. Like the Flash of Color exercise, the simplicity of noticing light was astounding to many students. One student had taken photography workshops and was used to "manipulating light" when they took indoor or portrait pictures. The Way of Light exercise—to *see* light as light—prompted them to capture images they would not have noticed before, such as the playful patterns of shadow on the wall right behind their computer screen as they were about to join a class via Zoom. Another student commented how the seeing light as light exercise opened up limitless ways of seeing the same object, from different angles and at different times of the day. This experience expanded how she *saw* others in her life. Her relations with others became less constricted and defined, but rather, rich with many possibilities.

Two students shared that they thought they would not be able to take many pictures of light when they could not find time to do this assignment until at dusk one day. But to their surprise, they *saw* light everywhere. One of them noticed light in the kitchen and took a picture of a piece of used aluminum foil reflecting glowing light with incredible pattern of texture. As they began to *see* light permeating in assumingly dark places, the binary notion of light and darkness was called into question. In fact, where there is light, there is shadow. Light and shadow reflect each other. Through this sight sensory awareness of the nonseparation of light and shadow, the grip of binary thinking began to loosen. I invited these two students to bring their embodied insight of nonduality further to see the interdependent quality of the world and the constructed and illusory boundary of "self" and "other."

After listening to his peers' sharing of their experience from the Way of Light exercise, one student aptly captured how simply *seeing* light as light connected them to the moment as it was—how the light showed up and how the image showed up, just as it was—rather than manipulating light or the image. Many students were amazed to *see* the extraordinary out of the ordinary when they maintained an open and receptive presence to what they *saw*, free of the agenda or expectation of the ego mind. The photo images were alive, vivid, and creative. "The most direct way to spontaneous creativity was not in breaking the rules," McQuade and Hall write. "It was in making contact with the world before there are rules at all. In Nalanda Miksang photography, we work with what we see. This comes before rules."[18]

This creative emergence students experienced in the Miksang photography exercise invigorated their open mind and receptive presence to each other in class. In a class space with students of very diverse social positionalities, the practice of holding space and suspending expectations, assumptions, or judgments is crucial for students to stay present and engaged in critical discussion about social justice issues. This is the "contemplative interaction" David Sable worked to cultivate in his classroom to enhance students' critical thinking to consider multiple points of view with a sense of connectedness based on taking "an uncertain journey together and risking the suspension of beliefs long enough to be challenged."[19]

Being willing and able to suspend assumptions or beliefs long enough during discussions of social justice issues is even more important in a remote learning space, as students may have less opportunity to know each other outside of the educational context. Sable found in his research on the impacts of contemplative practices on critical thinking that "connectedness supports critical thinking that is more focused on deeper and broader understanding than winning an argument. It opens the door to respect, empathy, and compassion: reason in service of the heart."[20] In a class of students of diverse identities and intersecting subjectivities of privilege and marginalization, students often engage in intense arguments not just because they want to win an argument, but more importantly, because of the harm and wounds from experiences of marginalization and social injustice. How to foster a sense of connectedness among students of such diverse subjectivities in a class requires a contemplative space where students are willing and able to maintain an open and receptive presence to what is challenging within and with each other.[21]

A CO-LEARNING COMMUNITY OF COLLECTIVE PRESENCE

What further supported students' shared sense of safety for vulnerability was the intentional creation of a co-learning community informed by Paulo Freire's work.[22] This pedagogical orientation is also shared by the Community of Inquiry framework in online education as discussed in Palalas and Dell's respective chapters in this volume. In this course, whether being held in person or online, I always dedicated the first fifteen to twenty minutes at the beginning of each class for checking in, asking students to share (sometimes verbally and sometimes via Zoom chat) how they were physically, emotionally, and/or mentally arriving in class. This was then followed by a short guided mindful breathing or movement exercise (in front of the computer screen) according to their physical, emotional, or mental state, to support them to arrive more fully in the learning space.

The next thirty to forty minutes would be students' sharing of their daily mindful walking experience over the past week. In the Zoom environment, students were asked to invite the next person to share after they finished. This small action often evoked a warm feeling of community among the students when they were invited by their peer to speak. Embodying the insight of interbeing, I emphasized to the students that they had multiple teachers in this course. First, they were their own teacher through their own direct embodied experience and insight from the daily mindfulness practice. Second, they learned from their peers in class who generously shared their experience and insight from the practice. Third, they learned from the readings and me as the course instructor. I, too, learned from my students' experience. Together, we were on a co-learning journey.

Inspired by Thich Nhat Hanh's teaching of interbeing, bell hooks writes in *Teaching Community: A Pedagogy of Hope*: "When we practice interbeing in the classroom, we are transformed not just by one individual's presence but by our collective presence. Experiencing the world of learning we can make together in community is the ecstatic moment that makes us come and come again to the present, to the now, to the place where we are real."[23]

So often, the weekly check-in sharing among students of their practice during the week brought forth deeper insights into their experience and the course materials. Students realized that they were not alone in their perceived "failure" or "mistakes" in the practice. There was a sense of relief in their shared struggles. It was not uncommon in the first couple of weeks to hear students talk about how they could not find time to practice, to pause and breathe, or felt awkward in walking slowly. Some worked hard to "get it right" and felt frustrated when they could not get what they expected, such as staying focused or feeling calmer. I invited them to also share what went through their mind when the practice did not go as well as they wished. As the students began to *see* what the mind told them about their practice or even who they were when they struggled with the practice, we often laughed at the "tricks" and sometimes "excuses" of the mind.

During the check-in sharing, students came alive and were fully engaged and connected to each other's joy from affirming practice experiences, silliness, or frustration with their perceived "mistakes" or "failures," and everything in between. They soon learned that all experiences were welcome in mindfulness. All were learning moments about their/our habits of the mind. There was space for everything. Slowly, students seemed to become more open to being real in their sharing and in holding space for each other's vulnerabilities.

CLOSING THOUGHTS

To close, I return to bell hooks's pedagogy of hope:

> Education is about healing and wholeness, about empowerment, liberation, transcendence, about renewing the vitality of life, about finding and claiming ourselves and our place in the world, to reclaim the sacred at the heart of knowing, teaching, and learning, to reclaim it from the depressive mode of knowing that honors only data, logic, analysis, and a systematic disconnection of self from the world, self from others.[24]

In this chapter, I share my experiment of a walking-based pedagogy, focusing on the Miksang photography exercises in the Mindful Walking Project, and the creation of a co-learning community through weekly check-in sharing among students on their experience from their mindfulness practice. It was a response to hooks's call for us as teacher to "create a sense of the sacred simply by the way we arrange the classroom, by the manner in which we teach" to "affirm our students that academic brilliance is not enhanced by disconnection"; rather, "we show that the student who is whole can achieve academic excellence."[25] In a remote learning environment, we are also called to be creative and whole in how we set up the online learning space, synchronously or asynchronously.

SACRED PAUSE

We can practice "sacred pause" with students in class online or in person every now and then to invite everyone, including ourselves, to come back to the body in the present moment. It is a sacred pause because it supports us to come back to our center and stay grounded. Below are some examples:

- When the class returns from a break (not just at the beginning of the class), in between lectures or discussion topics, we can invite everyone to take three deep breaths together or stand up and stretch.
- When we present our lecture PowerPoint slides via shared screen during a synchronous session or on recording for asynchronous viewing, we can bring in a slide with an image of nature in between the slides.[26] Invite the class to take a breath together to come back to the body and enjoy the nature image before continuing to the next slide or topic.
- We can invite students to take a breath and come back to the body (e.g., the felt sense of their hand, their feet, or the contact between their body and the chair) every now and then during the class discussion period so that we can fully take in what has just been discussed or shared. At times when there is a heated discussion, this sacred pause would also support us to sit with our reactivity with kindness and openness.
- Sacred pause in everyday life: I ask students to choose one mundane daily routine activity, such as opening a door, picking up your cell phone, starting the car, opening the fridge, etc. as their "bell of mindfulness."[27] Students practice three-breath before they engage in one of these activities consistently for a week. This helps support students to cultivate the habit of taking a "sacred pause" in their everyday life.

There are infinite ways to bring a "sacred pause" into our class. Be creative and have fun!

NOTES

1. Thich Nhat Hanh, *The Heart of the Buddha's Teaching: Transforming Suffering into Peace, Joy, and Liberation* (New York: Harmony, 1998).

2. Thich Nhat Hanh, *Peace Is Every Step: The Path of Mindfulness in Everyday Life* (New York: Bantam, 1992), 96.

3. In body-scan meditation, we bring our attention to different parts of the body, slowly moving from head to toes or from toes to head, feeling the sensations as we go and directing the breath into and out from the different parts. It can be performed while lying down, sitting, or in other postures. It helps bring the practitioner to the present moment in the body and reestablish connection with themselves.

4. Pohanna Pyne Feinberg, "Towards a Walking-Based Pedagogy," *Journal of the Canadian Association for Curriculum Studies* 14, no. 1 (November 25, 2016): 147–65, https://jcacs.journals.yorku.ca/index.php/jcacs/article/view/40312.

5. Ibid.

6. The Perspectivity Collective, "The Mindful Walking Project," *Perspectivity*, October 25, 2019, https://perspectivity.org/the-mindful-walking-project/.

7. Miksang Society for Contemplative Photography, "What Is Miksang?," Nalanda Miksang Society for Contemplative Photography, 2008, http://www.miksang.org/m/whatismiksang.html.

8. For a description of the tree contemplation exercise, refer to Yuk-Lin Renita Wong, "Returning to Silence, Connecting to Wholeness: Contemplative Pedagogy for Critical Social Work Education," *Journal of Religion & Spirituality in Social Work: Social Thought* 32, no. 3 (July 1, 2013): 277, doi:10.1080/15426432.2013.801748.

9. The soundscape exercises were intended to sensitize students' auditory awareness to the sonic environment. It can also be practiced as a sound meditation (Jon Kabat-Zinn, "Hearing," in *Coming to Our Senses: Healing Ourselves and the World Through Mindfulness*, New York: Hyperion, 2005, 202–4). Students were first asked to stay in a spot to draw a sound map (Sharing Nature Worldwide, "Sound Map," accessed October 7, 2022, https://www.sharingnature.com/sound-map.html). As students were more attuned to their sonic environment, they were asked to walk around in their neighborhood to record two of their favorite sounds (Unauthored, "'You Learn a Lot about the City by Asking about Its Sound': Peter Cusack Interview, Sounds," CDM Create Digital Music, May 21, 2013, https://cdm.link/2013/05/you-learn-a-lot-about-the-city-by-asking-about-its-sound-peter-cusack-interview/). Students found the soundscape exercises "ear-opening" to discover or connect to their neighborhood in a completely new way.

10. Lata Mani, *Interleaves: Ruminations on Illness and Spiritual Life* (New Delhi: Yoda Press, 2011), 88, https://www.amazon.ca/Interleaves-Ruminations-Illness-Spiritual-Life/dp/9380403186.

11. Henepola Gunaratana, *Mindfulness in Plain English* (Boston: Wisdom Publications, 2011), 132.

12. Shunryu Suzuki, *Zen Mind, Beginner's Mind* (New York: Weatherhill, Inc., 1995), 21.

13. Shari M. Geller and Leslie S. Greenberg, *Therapeutic Presence: A Mindful Approach to Effective Therapy* (Washington, DC: American Psychological Association, 2012), 185, doi:10.1037/13485-000.

14. Jo Mensinga and Loretta Pyles, "Embodiment: A Key to Social Workers' Wellbeing and Attainment of Social Justice," *Australian Social Work* 74, no. 2 (2021): 132, doi:10.1080/0312407X.2021.1858472.

15. Miksang Society for Contemplative Photography, "What Is Miksang?," Nalanda Miksang Society for Contemplative Photography, 2008, http://www.miksang.org/m/whatismiksang.html.

16. The Miksang Institute, "What Is Miksang?," Miksang Contemporary Photography, 2018, https://www.miksang.com/miksang/.

17. John McQuade and Miriam Hall, *Looking and Seeing: Nalanda Miksang Contemplative Photography—Way of Seeing*, vol. 1 (Madison, WI: Drala Publishing, 2015).

18. McQuade and Hall, *Looking and Seeing*, xiii.

19. David Sable, "Reason in the Service of the Heart: The Impacts of Contemplative Practices on Critical Thinking," *The Journal of Contemplative Inquiry* 1 (2014): 1.

20. Ibid., 1.

21. Also refer to the Sacred Pause textbox for the practice of "sacred pause" to support students to pause in the middle of class, to come back to their body, and to

fully take in what has been shared by their fellow classmates, or to recognize and sit with their reactivity in heated discussion before responding.

22. Antonia Darder, *Reinventing Paulo Freire: A Pedagogy of Love* (New York: Routledge, 2017), doi:10.4324/9781315560779; Paulo Freire, *Pedagogy of the Oppressed* (New York: Seabury Press, 1970); Peter Leonard, Paulo Freire, and Peter McLaren, eds., *Paulo Freire: A Critical Encounter* (London: Routledge, 1992), doi:10.4324/9780203420263.

23. bell hooks, *Teaching Community: A Pedagogy of Hope* (New York: Routledge, 2003), 173–74.

24. Ibid., 179–80.

25. Ibid., 180.

26. I learned this idea of inserting a nature image between PowerPoint slides in presentations from Marisela Gomez (https://www.mariselabgomez.com/), an activist and mindfulness teacher who has published numerous writings on mindfulness and racial justice.

27. Thich Nhat Hanh, *Peace Is Every Step: The Path of Mindfulness in Everyday Life*, 29.

BIBLIOGRAPHY

Darder, Antonia. *Reinventing Paulo Freire: A Pedagogy of Love*. New York: Routledge, 2017. doi:10.4324/9781315560779.

Feinberg, Pohanna Pyne. "Towards a Walking-Based Pedagogy." *Journal of the Canadian Association for Curriculum Studies* 14, no. 1 (November 25, 2016): 147–65. https://jcacs.journals.yorku.ca/index.php/jcacs/article/view/40312.

Freire, Paulo. *Pedagogy of the Oppressed*. New York: Seabury Press, 1970.

Geller, Shari M., and Leslie S. Greenberg. *Therapeutic Presence: A Mindful Approach to Effective Therapy*. Washington, DC: American Psychological Association, 2012. doi:10.1037/13485-000.

Gunaratana, Henepola. *Mindfulness in Plain English*. Boston: Wisdom Publications, 2011.

Hanh, Thich Nhat. *Peace Is Every Step: The Path of Mindfulness in Everyday Life*. New York: Bantam, 1992.

hooks, bell. *Teaching Community: A Pedagogy of Hope*. New York: Routledge, 2003.

Kabat-Zinn, Jon. "Hearing." In *Coming to Our Senses: Healing Ourselves and the World Through Mindfulness*, 202–4. New York: Hyperion, 2005.

Leonard, Peter, Paulo Freire, and Peter McLaren, eds. *Paulo Freire: A Critical Encounter*. London: Routledge, 1992. doi:10.4324/9780203420263.

Mani, Lata. *Interleaves: Ruminations on Illness and Spiritual Life*. New Delhi: Yoda Press, 2011.

McQuade, John, and Miriam Hall. *Looking and Seeing: Nalanda Miksang Contemplative Photography—Way of Seeing*. Vol. 1. Madison, WI: Drala Publishing, 2015.

Mensinga, Jo, and Loretta Pyles. "Embodiment: A Key to Social Workers' Wellbeing and Attainment of Social Justice." *Australian Social Work* 74, no. 2 (2021): 131–33. doi:10.1080/0312407X.2021.1858472.

Miksang Institute. "What Is Miksang?" Miksang Contemporary Photography, 2018. https://www.miksang.com/miksang/.

Miksang Society for Contemplative Photography. "What Is Miksang?" Nalanda Miksang Society for Contemplative Photography, 2008. http://www.miksang.org/m/whatismiksang.html.

Perspectivity Collective. "The Mindful Walking Project." *Perspectivity*, October 25, 2019. https://perspectivity.org/the-mindful-walking-project/.

Sable, David. "Reason in the Service of the Heart: The Impacts of Contemplative Practices on Critical Thinking." *The Journal of Contemplative Inquiry* 1 (2014): 1–22.

Sharing Nature Worldwide. "Sound Map." My Site. Accessed October 7, 2022. https://www.sharingnature.com/sound-map.html.

Suzuki, Shunryu. *Zen Mind, Beginner's Mind*. New York: Weatherhill, Inc., 1995.

——— *The Heart of the Buddha's Teaching: Transforming Suffering into Peace, Joy, and Liberation*. New York: Harmony, 1998.

Wong, Yuk-Lin Renita. "Returning to Silence, Connecting to Wholeness: Contemplative Pedagogy for Critical Social Work Education." *Journal of Religion & Spirituality in Social Work: Social Thought* 32, no. 3 (July 1, 2013): 269–85. doi:10.1080/15426432.2013.801748.

"'You Learn a Lot about the City by Asking about Its Sound': Peter Cusack Interview, Sounds." CDM Create Digital Music, May 21, 2013. https://cdm.link/2013/05/you-learn-a-lot-about-the-city-by-asking-about-its-sound-peter-cusack-interview/.

PAUSE

Get Up and Enjoy a Cup of Tea (or your favorite drink)

Chapter Ten

Hardwired for Presence in an Online World

A Contemplative Perspective and Practice Guide for Educators

Charles Scott, Heesoon Bai, and Laurie Anderson

On the Saturday morning of class in our master's of education contemplative inquiry program, we were having our usual morning check-in. Although our classes were now online because of the pandemic, the check-in was still in practice. Check-ins, which can sometimes last thirty to forty-five minutes, or longer, are an opportunity for students and faculty to check in within themselves and with each other, typically conducted in a circle, participants facing each other: "What am I feeling and sensing right now? What thoughts are visiting me? What is surfacing for me at this time? How am I doing?" No one interrupts or verbally responds while the person is speaking; the individual has the full attention of the group. It is a check-in that acknowledges and gives voice to body, mind, heart, and spirit.

On that Saturday morning, our check-in went even deeper. When it came to Tom's[1] turn, he spoke up about the depression he had been experiencing and the challenges it was presenting, tearfully relating what he had been feeling and witnessing. It was impossible for me not to be deeply moved, and looking at others' facial expressions, I sensed that others were similarly affected.

When he finished, there was clearly an empathic pause as we absorbed what he had so bravely and openly related. Then, Tara, one of the other students, spoke. "I'm wondering if we could have a short break so everyone can go and get a cup of tea and then we come back just to hold space for Tom." Her suggestion was enthusiastically embraced, and so we did.

When we all reassembled a few minutes later, Tara explained how tea was used in Indigenous communities, both as a coming-of-age ceremony and also during difficult times, to hold space for each other. We then just hung out together online, mostly in silence, quietly sipping our tea. There was the occasional, supportive comment, but mostly there was just us, students and faculty, silently being together, silently being community. We hung out together for almost an hour.² That was the curriculum. We later dubbed this "Tea with Tom," and students remarked that it was one of the most meaningful experiences of the entire course; months later, they remarked it was one of the most meaningful experiences of the entire two-year program. We were, simply and profoundly, both being present for and with Tom, and allowing Tom to be fully present, to be fully accepted by us. This is the power of presence.

Martin Buber, author of *I and Thou*, wrote in an essay on dialogue that out of a personal experience of his, when a young man came to him in deep existential need, he later reflected: "He had come to me, he had come in this hour. What do we expect when we are in despair and yet go to a man [*sic*]? Surely a presence by means of which we are told that nevertheless there is meaning." He goes on to add, "I know no fulness but each mortal hour's fulness of claim and responsibility."³

HARDWIRED FOR PRESENCE

Our time as learners and teachers since the start of the COVID-19 pandemic has opened up to the realities of a volatile, uncertain, complex, and ambiguous (VUCA) world.⁴ Not only have we had curricular uncertainty, but also, with the move to online spaces, pedagogical uncertainty, as well (not to mention the uncertainties and angst of assessment!).

We have found in our work that students appreciate—in the best of times, but especially now—a teacher who is present for what Kazantzakis in *Zorba the Greek* refers to as "the whole catastrophe": a teacher who is capable of being unperturbed, grounded, and centered, thus being present not only to the whole catastrophe, but also to the students in a receptive manner, offering as well as receiving fully. Presence as awareness to the fullness of the present moment, within and without. Presence includes, but is much more than, a mindful awareness; more importantly, presence is an ontological grounding in being. We suggest that the possibility and potentials of presence are very much possible in online educational settings.

Our first thesis is that we are "hardwired" for presence, both subjectively and intersubjectively. Our second thesis is that the hardwired capacity for presence can be expansively developed appropriately with sensitivity to the contexts, such as the online environment under discussion in this chapter. Combined, these two theses build up our case-making that presence for teaching and learning is vital in an online environment, and can be expansively cultivated. This chapter explores both theses in depth.

As well, we will discuss both the subjective and intersubjective dimensions of teacher presence. We will also review how we might develop these subjective and intersubjective elements of our being, allowing us to be more fully present with and for our students, allowing presence to develop in and through the relationships we have with them and others.

The Subjective Grounding of Presence: Inner Presence

Presence matters, regardless of whether our teaching and learning occurs physically face-to-face or in online settings. There is, understandably, a tendency to assume that online environments do not allow presence, at least not easily, unlike the "real" face-to-face environments. We the authors of this chapter disagree, based on our own teaching experiences of recent years. In these online settings of Zoom, Teams, or Collaborate, we have found that teachers can manifest a presence that serves as a catalyst to promote both connectivity and learning; the manifestation of a full, embodied, heartfelt sense of presence helps to create the dialogical ethos that promotes deeper and more engaged learning.

What is our evidence for these claims? It is limited to the online class experience based on each of us three co-authors of this paper teaching graduate seminar courses to around 20 students in each class over the past two years, along with some 120 undergraduate students. That works out to be our combined experience of teaching, roughly, 240 students. Even so, our "data" would qualify as "anecdotal." However, the central argument we present is based on the philosophical understanding that presence is a phenomenon inherent in who we are as conscious and aware beings. As such, *presence can be manifest in any ontic environment*, whether virtual or face-to-face.

From a subjective perspective, presence is a mindful, conscious awareness of self, a sense of self, along with the conscious manifestation or expression of that sense of self in one's beingness and actions. Genoud defines presence, from a Buddhist perspective, as "being conscious of being conscious of something";[5] for Genoud, presence and meditative presence are, substantively, one and the same: Presence denotes the consciousness aware of itself. As a side remark here, we add that, as our experience would show, there can be varying degrees of presence, depending on the degrees of self-awareness and the abilities to manifest or express that self. We will build on this point later.

For us, the authors, presence is an aware, holistic sense of self. It is an awareness of self that has somatic, aesthetic, emotional, intellectual, moral, energetic, relational, and spiritual dimensions; in short, it includes all aspects of our being and our awareness of this holistically grounded self, what poet John O'Donahue refers to as the "whole atmosphere of a person."[6]

The person of presence knows who they are and they know that they know. (As an aside, authenticity is both one of the manifestations of presence and a vehicle to its manifestation.) Senge, Scharmer, Jaworski, and Flowers appreciate presence not only as being aware of the present moment but also as "deep listening, of being open beyond one's preconceptions and historical ways of making sense. . . . leading to a state of 'letting come.'"[7]

Pedagogically speaking, presence is a manifestation of the teacher's whole being, brought intentionally into the learning setting.[8] For Kessler, three qualities above all contribute to teaching presence: respectful discipline, an open heart, and presence itself. Presence denotes being fully open to the present moment, being free of baggage and concerns that are not pertinent to the situation, being responsive to the moment and its needs, being flexible enough to respond to present needs and the "teachable moment," being creative and imaginative in the moment, and humble enough to realize that you are always learning. Finally, she notes that presence is developed through the courage we show in our willingness to be dropped "into the cauldron of our own emotional and spiritual growth."[9]

In her work on teacher presence, Mary O'Reilley points to the contemplative discipline and challenges associated with presence:

> The discipline of presence requires me to *be there*, with my senses focused on the group at hand, listening rather than thinking about what I'm going to say—observing the students, the texts, and the sensory world of the classroom. This is harder than *zazen*. In *zazen*, nobody talks back to you. . . . Hospitality . . . implies reception of the challenging and unfamiliar.[10]

There is not only the requirement to "be there," but also to care, to offer hospitality. Ted Aoki expands on the notion of presence as a manifestation of a state of being that manifests care. Presence, he writes, is the "beingness of teaching," adding that teaching through being "is attuned to the place where care dwells, a place of ingathering and belonging, where the in-dwelling of teachers and students is made possible by the presence of care that each has for the other."[11] From these authors, we also see a particularized sense of being that is grounded in an ethic of care and hospitality.

We now come to the intersections of being and doing. Miller[12] points to the idea that presence is a noun, not a verb, a state of being, not doing. And yet, while we would agree, we would also suggest that dichotomizing being and doing is neither realistic nor helpful. In truth, if our doing lacks presence, what we have is unconscious doing: robotic and "soulless." Presence is dynamic. It can figure into everything we are and do. It is active, responsive, thus reflecting the ongoing growth of the individual. It exists in the seemingly paradoxical tension of being and doing, each informing the other in an ongoing dynamic.

O'Donahue refers to the "flow of soul"[13] in describing presence and the art of "belonging to one's soul that keeps one's presence aflame."[14] The flow of soul represents this dynamic aspect of presence, its manifestations in doing that are born out of being.

Cohen[15] also speaks to this dynamism in referring to listening with ears, mind, and heart; presence then can become the "greatest gift a person can offer."[16] Presence thus becomes a manifestation of our ongoing efforts in being aware, centered, attuned to in-the-moment context, and relationally responsive. Doing informs being, while being makes the doing conscious and self-aware; it makes the doing possible. Presence is both developing through contemplation and, at the same time, becomes the contemplative expression of who we are, grounded in the fullness of being and awareness. Presence may be said to represent one of the aspects of praxis in the teacher's life, reflecting the intersections of both being and doing, theory and practice.

THE INTERSUBJECTIVE GROUNDING OF PRESENCE: INTER-PRESENCE

Mayes has characterized teaching presence as being "so mindful of the moment that it uniquely embraces each student in the class and draws him or her into sacred moments of presence—presence to oneself, to each other, and to the subject at hand."[17] This characterization highlights two things. First, the *quality* of awareness, which we have noted. Second, there is the *recognition* of relationality: to others and to the subject at hand. There is a clear intersubjective dimension to presence. That is, presence is not something that just belongs, and is confined, to the self, as if it is a private property. Like air or water, it belongs to the Whole, dynamically infusing all that constitutes the whole.

We suggest that presence manifests more fully as we expand our sense of self, transcending the cognitive and cultural limitations of being solely identified with one, limited body, isolated from others. Presence has an expansive, reaching-out, and melding quality. The boundaries of self expand and become more porous; there is a lessening of the boundary between I and not-I. The development of presence can mirror the expansion of self to a more universal, interconnected Self. In its greatest manifestations, this greater sense of presence represents a movement of self to Self (or, from a Buddhist perspective, to "no self").[18] As Thich Nhat Hanh puts it:

> The first notion we need to throw away is the notion of self. There is the idea that I am this body, this body is me, or, this body is mine and belongs to me. We say these things based on the notion that "I am." But a better statement would

be, "I inter-am." It's closer to the truth in the light of interconnectedness; we see there is no separate self that can exist by itself.[19]

As Thich Nhat Hanh put it later, "You cannot just be by yourself alone. You have to inter-be with every other thing."[20] As Emerson states, poetically, "There is one animal, one plant, one matter and one force."[21] Contemplative practices and approaches exist that work in this domain of interbeing.[22]

Miller writes that, as we noted earlier, presence manifests phenomenologically as "unmediated presence." He adds: "When we experience Presence, duality drops away, and as teachers, we see ourselves in our students. At the deepest level, we may experience brief moments of communion with our students."[23] The interconnected, intersubjective dimension of presence allows one, to paraphrase from the words of Pete Townshend's (1969) song, to see the other, feel the other, touch the other, and heal the other.[24] This dimension of presence opens us up to the relational aspects of being.

Over decades of work, Martin Buber developed a relational model of being, best known through the phrasing of the *I-Thou* relationship. The significance of Buber's argument is that both *I* and *Thou* come into being through dialogical engagements; that is, we are not fully human until we come into dialogical relationships with others. As Buber writes in *I and Thou*: "I become through my relation to the *Thou*; as I become *I*, I say *Thou*."[25]

"Becoming a self" is a relational process, but the corollary is also true: bringing a full presence to the engagement contributes to it becoming a dialogue. The engagement with the other who is apprehended as *Thou*—which is seen as boundless, whole, connected, and sacred—is thus necessary for the formation of our *I-ness*. Buber points out that the "real, filled present"[26] is made manifest by each individual bringing fullness of being, by then encountering each other, and thereby developing a relationship.

Thus, I come to the encounter with presence, and through my committed engagement I place myself squarely in the here and now, in the meeting with the other: This is a moral commitment. To the degree that I place myself thusly, the present remains something that is "continually present and enduring." Coming into presence thus involves both a moral and spiritual commitment. Later in *I and Thou*, Buber adds:

> He listens to what is emerging from himself, to the course of being in the world; not in order to be supported by it, but in order to bring it to reality as it desires, in its need of him, to be brought—with human spirit and deed, human life and death. I said *he believes*, but that really means he meets.[27]

All of this combines to bring into being the dialogical turning toward another, the meeting with another, the manifestation of intersubjective presence.

To repeat the quintessential line from Cohen: "Giving full presence to another is, I believe, the greatest gift a person can offer."[28] Life beckons for our presence: we are called to give meaningful response.

When we recognize others and our responsive and responsible relation to them, we come into awareness of our relation to a larger "Present Being," which opens us to the world, and the spirit.[29] The overall significance here is twofold. First, the teacher's presence is made more fully possible through dialogical engagement with another, who is seen as *Thou*; the other as *Thou* contributes to our coming into presence. Thus, presence represents a dynamic, intersubjective unfolding. Buber writes: "For the inmost growth of the self is not accomplished . . . in [one's] relation to himself [*sic*], but in the relation between the one and the other . . . pre-eminently in the mutuality of making present."[30]

As the lyrics of a song composed by Pete Townshend in 1978 question, "Who are you? I really wanna know."[31] As educators, who we are is important. You cannot fake it in a classroom: Students will "have your number" in only a few seconds of first meeting you.

As Palmer writes: "Teaching, like any truly human activity, emerges from one's inwardness, for better or worse. As I teach, I project the condition of my soul onto my students, my subject, and our way of being together."[32] Good teaching comes, Palmer asserts, from the "identity and integrity of the teacher";[33] this includes expressions of authentic vulnerability.

The generative dialogic relationship referred to above often requires the teacher to model the vulnerability and presence desired in each student. Indeed, a teacher's intentionality to be fully present—open, vulnerable, and embracing the moment—creates the trusted "container" that encourages students to engage deeply and authentically.

During the pandemic, a couple of us were teaching an undergraduate, introductory course on education, one that is often taken by students from many other faculties. Knowing the anxiety students were feeling, and mindful of the guidance our university president had offered faculty and staff—"Above all, kindness and compassion," we offered a laid-back atmosphere. We'd start off sharing really bad jokes and just chilling with one another. We could see these efforts had the desired effect.

But, as well, we made sure we offered students lots of opportunities to share their ideas and visions of education, informing them that we honored their decades of educational experience and insight. Sadly, too often in the academy, even as we focus on equity, diversity, and inclusion, we fail to legitimate the students' knowing, instead privileging the knowledge represented in various "texts"—readings, videos, and so on. We wanted to give the students voice. We wanted them to develop presence and be honored for it.

And they loved it. They had a lot to say. We developed an exciting community of inquiry, a dynamic process of community. We were keenly aware that the facts, readings, and other "curriculum" materials were in fact less important than the pedagogical environment—the community ethos of attunement, empathy, and caring we wished to create. The pedagogy in many ways does and will represent the curriculum and will be what the students remember. In end-of-term feedback, one student wrote: "Everyone should have this experience at least once at university, to know what is possible. I wish it could be the experience in every course."

In recalling the "Tea with Tom" vignette, what was so meaningful for the students was this intersubjective connectivity, this sense of silent communion. It represented for them a new sense of identity, one bound in relationality, what Wilber has referred to as the "nexus of a we."[34] Moreover, the experience represented the shift in curricular orientation we had been promoting in the program, from "content" to "process," and, beyond that, to an understanding that process is subtle but powerful; the building of an intimately connected community was in fact the very content our program envisioned. The community had its grounding in being present with and for one another. Furthermore, the boundaries between student and teacher blurred, representing what Freire has called the "student–teacher contradiction."[35]

THE INNER WORK OF DEVELOPING PRESENCE

We mentioned earlier that presence is an ontological grounding in being. Presence is a native—even if partially obscured or hidden—part of our being, in both its subjective and intersubjective dimensions; it literally is the fullest manifestation of who we are. We can bring presence into greater manifestation as we make connection with the subjective and intersubjective dimensions of presence. For Kessler, "cultivating presence is both a psychological and spiritual path"[36] requiring commitment to that ongoing work of development.

Contemplative work in developing an awareness of the self is valuable in developing presence. Our argument is that contemplative work allows us to work with or reveal the capacities that are inherently parts of our being. As we noted above, Genoud[37] points to the Buddhist contemplative practice of being conscious of consciousness, of developing that meta-awareness; such a practice is common to a number of contemplative traditions.

This consciousness of consciousness is, as an instance, the essence of mindfulness practice. Significantly, Thich Nhat Hanh[38] points to the importance of an integrated approach when considering contemplative practices, and it is worth noting that the contemplative practices of most of the wisdom traditions are set within the context of a comprehensive, integrated approach to spiritual development.[39] Thich Nhat Hanh points out, for example, that mindfulness practice needs to be considered, along with "Full Awareness in Breathing," and he outlines a version of the traditional meditation practice of focusing on the incoming and outgoing breath that is to be undertaken alongside traditional mindfulness practices.[40]

As we see above in Thich Nhat Hanh's emphasis on awareness of breaths, presence also has somatic and phenomenological elements. The person who manifests presence is grounded, both literally and metaphorically, feeling grounded in the body and connected to the earth in the present moment. Ray points to the significance of embodiment in being awake, aware, and present:

> To be awake, to be enlightened, is to be fully and completely embodied. To be fully embodied means to be at one with who we are, in every respect, including our physical being, our emotions, and the totality of our karmic situation. It is to be entirely present to who we are and to the journey of our becoming.[41]

Ray (2008) offers contemplative practices that "entail approaching, entering, exploring, and fully fathoming the body,"[42] working with both the surface of the body and its phenomenological manifestations within; as well, the contemplative work includes working with the subtle energies of the body (*prana* or *qi*). Ray's work is an example (one of many in the contemplative traditions) of working to realize a grounding, a gaining of presence, in and through the body, to both the earth and thus to all other beings.

We thus avoid the trap of restricting contemplative practice to a purely mental operation, ignoring the body. Ray adds that working with the body includes an unconditional awareness of our emotions; presence is realized contemplatively through an integrated approach that includes the body, emotions, aesthetics, intellect, energetic systems, intuition, morals, and the spiritual dimensions of our being. In developing presence contemplatively, we can work with the body *and* our inner, phenomenological awareness of what the body reveals, of how the body grounds and connects us.

THE INTER-WORK OF DEVELOPING PRESENCE

Working with the body brings us to the intersubjective and interrelational dimensions of presence; the body not only grounds us but connects us to others and the world. There is, as Abram (1996) puts it, "an inescapable affinity, or affiliation, between other bodies and one's own. . . . By an associative 'empathy,' the embodied subject comes to recognize these other bodies as other centers of experience, other subjects."⁴³ We now live in and are capable of grounding our presence in a "collective landscape." We are now aware that our beingness is, inescapably, intersubjective; there is the "interweaving of our individual phenomenal fields into a single, ever-shifting fabric, a single phenomenological world or 'reality.'"⁴⁴

Ray echoes this point in asserting that one's sense of self—and, we would suggest, one's sense of presence—is linked to others and to the natural world. Our embodied contemplative experience awakens an intersubjective presence. We would stress that even in online environments, we connect somatically through sight and sound; two of our senses are thus engaged, sending and receiving messages and cues through which presence is or can be established.

> To be embodied, to be in the body, is to be in connection with everything. . . .
> To be in the body is to feel our connectedness with other people as subjects. It is to know the natural world, the earth and ocean, the rivers and mountains, as our relatives, others with whom we are in deep relation.⁴⁵

Indigenous contemplative approaches have long recognized the intersubjective dimensions of presence. Kelly notes that Indigenous epistemologies acknowledge the lifelong journey to completeness. In that journey, we "gift" to others our essence, our presence; in turn, we receive the essences of others. "This profound reciprocal sense that '*we* are all related, we *are* all related, we are *all* related, we are all *related*' is central to Indigenous ways of knowing, being and participating in the world."⁴⁶

Wagamese writes of this Indigenous perspective: "In this stillness, I am the trees alive with singing. I am the sky everywhere at once. I am the snow and the wind bearing stories across geographies and generations. I am the light everywhere descending."⁴⁷ Later he writes "ALL my relations. That means every person, just as it means every rock, mineral, blade of grass, and creature."⁴⁸ Wagamese is portraying intersubjective manifestations of presence.

There is a connection to what Buber (2000) refers to as the "Present Being" that ties all things together; it is the connective spirit that is both immanent and yet transcends creation. That connection is made possible when I come to see the other as *Thou*; the recognition of *Thou* is not to see the other as an object, but as a subject who is "whole in himself [*sic*], he is Thou and fills the heavens."⁴⁹

In the scenario we presented at the beginning of this chapter, the student who was present with the one who had shared his experience of depression was able to manifest this presence—which was a teaching presence, since she taught all of us—manifesting the qualities we mention above. She had that "inescapable affinity" and "associate empathy" Abram mentions; there was that interweaving of individual phenomenal fields.

She had the grounded, somatic connection Ray points to, even though we were in an online environment—an embodied presence. She offered what Kelly refers to as a gift of her essence. All of this was accepted by Tom. All of this brought us together into a deeper community of presence, more fully alive, through these qualities, to one another.

In the classroom setting where our cohort program is situated, a suite of deliberative dialogues and actions are used to foster presence. These include but are not limited to beginning every session with a period of meditation ("connecting in silence"); a "checking-in" process, where heartfelt, open comments are encouraged and modeled; making space for laughter, and emerging moments of joy and sorrow (often avoided, ignored, or overlooked in classroom contexts); and encouraging dialogue and input among and between students and instructor. These are the building blocks of the safe, open, and trusting intersubjective "container" that cultivates authentic and sustained presence, even in an online learning environment.

DEVELOPING PRESENCE IN THE CLASSROOM

Allow me (Heesoon) to share with you my anonymized "live and learn" story. While conducting my classes via Zoom is not my favorite thing to do, at this point, I know I can do a very decent job, having taught several courses via Zoom. I do know, however, what the limitations and disadvantages are, at least for me, as well as what the strengths and advantages are for using Zoom. Taking what I'd come to know into account, by experience, in devising a pedagogy and conducting my classroom made a huge difference. Live and learn! But I had to learn this the hard way.

The graduate class that I was team-teaching with a colleague was unusually large; most students signed up for the course were brand-new in the program; I was new to using Zoom for teaching; and I really have never been too tech-savvy.

The previous time I'd taught this particular course was in person, and my colleague and I had had a wonderful and fulfilling experience teaching the class. As a group, we had bonded quickly and strongly, especially over and through a lot of experiential and embodied learning opportunities we created. Spontaneity and creativity, risk-taking in learning, and academic camaraderie were all in action week after week. It was most gratifying to watch our graduate students growing immensely and quite rapidly, intellectually, emotionally, and socially.

For me, the contrast in experience between the Zoom class and the in-person class the previous year was unimaginably stark. Each student's face was postage-stamp-sized on my screen. Interacting with students on my screen, I realized just how much I relied, in my in-person class, on visual cues coming from their whole and real body in motion and vibration, and including, of course, their facial expressions in terms of responding to them. There were continuous streams of such communication, much of which was not about content ideas that associated with course content. Rather, the communication was about our sense of security, safety, connection, empathy, sympathy, attunement, friendship, care, trust, and so on. I had a big difficulty identifying these cues in the context of the Zoom class environment.

When there were challenging dynamics among students in this Zoom class, I was unable to intervene promptly and decisively for the simple reason that I was fumbling for keys that would allow me to call people's attention to the interaction. As well, trying to find my colleague on Zoom to privately chat, to try to send a text message to a student, and so on, were all confounding for me in this Zoom class experience.

When, in fact, an altercation took place, due to one student's high reactivity level, I was unable to intervene in the rapid way that I would and could in an in-person environment, let alone prevent the escalation of reactivity. A little later, when the crisis seemed to have subsided, I looked for the student who was in reactive distress but couldn't see them. I realized that this person had exited the Zoom call and left the class, without any notice.

Stunned, my sense of presence was shot. Having taught for twenty-seven years, during which time I had learned to handle, with increasing skillfulness, all manner and degree of conflict and other dynamics arising in class, this challenging experience, plus its rather ugly aftermath, were extremely distressing for me. Nonetheless, this eye-opening experience taught me a lot about Zoom teaching: what to do, what to expect, what not to do, and how to set up the Zoom class and prepare the participants so that we could still have a solid learning and interpersonal experience.

In-person teaching is, for me, much more embodied and multidimensional, enabling me to respond to unexpected situations with speed and deftness, without losing contact with students, and also without losing my composure or presence of mind. I believe that a skilled teacher can "spread" attention so that he or she can attend to and keep track of many students nearly simultaneously, and respond to and take care of what's happening, even if just with a nod that signals "I am on your side," a smile that comforts and relaxes the student, an encouraging gesture that gives a gentle push to a hesitant student, or a serious look that signals a firm "stoplight" intervention, and so on. The Zoom environment deprives me of these embodied and fast responses and resonances.

The Zoom environment potentially deprives us of embodied and multisensorial communicative responses that are part of being fully present. In compensation, then, what I, Heesoon, have done is to set up a basic communication protocol that I ask all participating students (and myself, as the instructor) in my class to subscribe to and abide by when they are on Zoom. The protocol includes dialogue instructions on how to relate to each other, how to communicate with each other verbally and in the chat box, and, most important of all, how to constantly keep one's self-awareness "online" so as to check in with and become aware of one's own thoughts, feelings, and sensations while simultaneously interacting with others on Zoom. In this way, we increase the potential for all participants to maintain their presence and work toward quality communication in all the ways that we would hope for, no matter the environment. The principles and practices we have outlined in this chapter are what we have discovered works well to create a teaching presence, one that allows all to come into a greater sense of presence and educational agency.

CLOSING THOUGHTS

There is no formula for the development of a teaching presence. There is no "prescription." Teaching presence, whether it manifests in online or face-to-face environments, is a manifestation of being—and becoming. Becoming is the work of establishing beingness. To reiterate our three primary points:

1. Presence is an essential part of who we are; we are hardwired for presence.
2. That presence can be unfolded, developed through our sensitivity to and aliveness in various contexts, one of which would be an online context.
3. Sensitivity and aliveness can be developed through inner and inter work. Both inner and inter work become the ongoing, always active, work of becoming.

We assert that education fulfills its mandate to learners when it creates opportunities for them, as teachers and students, to come into fuller manifestations of presence. It requires us as educators to be sensitive to the uniqueness of each student, to be sensitive to each student's needs and longings, and to create conditions where students can grapple with existential questions, unfoldings, and realities.

In an age where reductionist performance requirements are still prominent, we may be required to defend the significance of a focus on coming into presence. The development of a sense of presence will necessarily involve a dynamic, reciprocal unfolding between student and teacher. There is, as we mentioned previously, also an ethic of care that underlines our engagements.

We bring our awareness of awareness into the here-and-now of teaching practice. O'Reilley gets it exactly right: In teaching practice, manifesting presence requires one to "*be there*," fully alive not only to one's consciousness but to the present moment.[50] We are alert to shifting dynamics moment to moment and the need to remain vigilant.

Contemplative practice as presence provides a way of negotiating the clamor of such spaces with a presence "so mindful of the moment that it uniquely embraces each student in the class and draws him or her into sacred moments of presence—presence to oneself, to each other, and to the subject at hand."[51] Regardless of the stated curricular subject matter, the subject at hand is always twofold.

First, creating opportunities where both students and teachers can come into full presence; it is then that teaching and learning become alive, meaningful, and authentic. Practically, this may require us to change our pedagogical practices, focusing less on "delivering content" and more on focusing on process, by which we mean devoting time to interacting with students to attend to their concerns, questions, and longings. In such interactions, students are able to express themselves fully, meaningfully. Such expressions are more likely when we are open, receptive, and caring.

Second is awakening into and maintaining an awareness of context, the situatedness of both students and teachers. Jalāl al-Dīn Rumi expresses this profoundly in his poem "Special Plates," translated by Coleman Barks in his book *The Essential Rumi*.[52] The poem repeatedly exhorts us to "notice": notice how others have arrived from personal and unique journeys; how there are dances of giving and taking; how different streams all flow into and connect eventually with one ocean; how each person has different needs and desires ("foods"), and that there are "chefs" preparing these "special plates," according to their needs. We as educators can prepare these special plates; we can feed our students well to the degree that we develop such awareness, develop our noticing. This is the aim of contemplative practice.

Our relational, intersubjective manifestation of presence includes our awareness of context, of the sociocultural, historical, economic, political, and environmental dynamics that shape our students, and us. Forbes, in his examination of mindfulness and its discontents, writes of a linkage between mindfulness and the prophetic, the demand that mindfulness itself "wakes up from its individualistic, self-absorbed approach and . . . on emergent ground, [embodies] a moral, social, universal transformative stance and action in society for the sake of all beings."[53] Forbes calls for contemplative practices that embody reflection, challenging and changing ourselves and our institutions as we move toward justice for all. That is, our contemplative practices must not only focus on the subjective but also on the intersubjective and interrelational, the objective and institutional.

As noted earlier, presence is ultimately a way of being, a disposition marked by how one relates to one's self and to others, importantly, in the present unvarnished moment, without artifice or contrivance. We can be there *with* our students, metaphorically alongside them, even in an online environment. Even when we are in an online environment, we do not stop being bodies, with senses, being grounded in the present moment, and paying attention to what emerges. In an online classroom, we can be as fully present to our students' needs and concerns as we might be in an in-person classroom. Our words, the tenor of our speech, our body language, even if reduced to the sight of our heads, can convey our being present to, and with, our students; they, in turn, can be fully present to us.

There are undoubtedly challenges in the online classroom—the Zoom session in which students have their cameras turned off, or in which there are several screens of students and it takes time to scroll through them all to notice everyone. We cannot do it all by ourselves, and we may need to take the time to try to ensure that we see every student and attend to their different needs. This is our point: The process of engagement is the content. The time spent in noticing, attending, caring, and responding is what will have an impact on students, will be what students remember.

Students crave authenticity and authentic meeting. They know the inauthentic and can spot it almost instantly. Regardless of the learning environment, we are required to show up as fully as possible.

We pointed earlier to the dynamics and intersections of being and doing. We emphasize that presence is developed and established through commitment and practice. The contemplative ways of developing presence are made possible, just as any other fruits of contemplation, through regular, committed, and patient practice—both personal and pedagogical. Again, all of this operates no differently in an online environment.

We acknowledge that the transition from the physical to the virtual for classrooms can be challenging and can present difficulties and problems for both students and teachers. Time and skills are needed; so is the understanding of our students and their needs, and the contexts we develop by noticing. Part of this understanding is what we have endeavored to establish in this chapter: the phenomenology of presence. As well, we have emphasized the importance of cultivating and developing presence for education. While presence as fundamental human capacity is "hardwired" into us, like breathing, developing it into an expanded and refined ability to deliver, share, infuse, presence is something that needs cultivation and development, particularly in the technology-based, online environments that have represented "disruptive" learning environments for our students.

NOTES

1. Pseudonyms are used here. We thank the students for their permission to use this vignette and for their helpful edits to this recounting.

2. Charles Scott, "Hanging Out: One of the High Arts of Dialogue," *SFU Educational Review* 3 (2009). https://doi.org/10.21810/sfuer.v3i.343.

3. Martin Buber, *Between Man and Man*, trans. Ronald Smith (London: Routledge, 2002), 16.

4. Warren Bennis and Burt Nanus, *Leaders: The Strategies for Taking Charge* (New York: Harper & Row, 1985); Linor Hadar, Oren Ergas, Bracha Alpert, and Tamar Ariav, "Rethinking Teacher Education in a VUCA World: Student Teachers' Social-Emotional Competencies During the Covid-19 Crisis," *European Journal of Teacher Education 43*, no. 4 (2020): 573–86; Paul LeBlanc, "Higher Education in a VUCA world," *Change: The Magazine of Higher Learning*, 50, nos. 3–4 (2018), 23–26.

5. Charles Genoud, "On the Cultivation of Presence in Buddhist Meditation," *Journal of Consciousness Studies* 16, nos. 10–11 (2009): 124.

6. John O'Donahue, *Eternal Echoes: Exploring our Yearning to Belong* (New York: HarperCollins, 1999), 53.

7. Peter Senge, Otto Scharmer, Joseph Jaworski, and Betty Flowers, *Presence: An Exploration of Profound Change in People, Organizations, and Society* (New York: Currency, 2005), 13–14.

8. Rachel Kessler, "The Teaching Presence," *Holistic Education Review* 4, no. 4 (1991): 4–15.

9. Kessler, "The Teaching Presence," 14.

10. Mary O'Reilley, *Radical Presence: Teaching as Contemplative Practice* (Portsmouth, NH: Boynton/Cook Publishers, 1998), 9.

11. Ted Aoki, "Layered Voices of Teaching: The Uncannily Correct and the Elusively True," in *Understanding Curriculum as Phenomenological and Deconstructed Text*, eds. William Pinar and William Reynolds (New York: Teachers College Press, 1992), 21.

12. John Miller, *The Contemplative Practitioner: Meditation in Education and the Workplace*, 2nd ed. (Toronto: University of Toronto Press, 2014).

13. O'Donohue, *Eternal Echoes: Exploring our Yearning to Belong*, 54.

14. Ibid., 66.

15. Avraham Cohen is a close colleague of the authors of this chapter, and we credit him for personally introducing the "check-in ritual" to us as an essential part of the contemplative pedagogy we can practice in all our educational settings.

16. Avraham Cohen, *Gateway to the Dao-Field: Essays for the Awakening Educator* (Amherst, NY: Cambria Press, 2009), 38.

17. Clifford Mayes, "The Use of Contemplative Practices in Teacher Education," *Encounter: Education for Meaning and Social Justice* 11 no. 3 (1998): 21.

18. Rupert Gethin, *The Foundations of Buddhism* (Oxford: Oxford University Press, 1998); Thich Nhat Hanh, *Beyond the Self: Teachings on the Middle Way*

(Berkeley, CA: Parallax Press, 2009); Thich Nhat Hanh, *Awakening of the Heart: Essential Buddhist Sutras and Commentaries* (Berkeley, CA: Parallax Press, 2012).

19. Hanh, *Beyond the Self: Teachings on the Middle Way*, x.

20. Hanh, *Awakening of the Heart: Essential Buddhist Sutras and Commentaries*, 4.

21. Ralph Waldo Emerson, *Poetry and Imagination* (Boston: James R. Osgood and Co., 1876), 9.

22. Olen Gunnlaugson, Charles Scott, Heesoon Bai, Ed Sarath, eds. *The Intersubjective Turn: Theoretical Approaches to Contemplative Learning and Inquiry Across Disciplines* (Albany: SUNY Press, 2017); Olen Gunnlaugson, Charles Scott, Heesoon Bai, Ed Sarath, eds. *Catalyzing the Field: Second-Person Approaches to Contemplative Learning and Inquiry.* (Albany: SUNY Press, 2019).

23. Miller, *The Contemplative Practitioner: Meditation in Education and the Workplace*, 26.

24. Pete Townshend, "See Me, Feel Me" (Decca/Track Records, 1969).

25. Martin Buber, *I and Thou*, trans. Ronald Smith, (New York: Scribner, 2000), 26.

26. Buber, *I and Thou*, 27.

27. Ibid., 64–65.

28. Cohen, *Gateway to the Dao-Field: Essays for the Awakening Educator*, 38.

29. Buber, *Between Man and Man*, 117.

30. Martin Buber, *The Knowledge of Man: Selected Essays*, trans. Ronald Smith and Maurice Friedman (New York: Harper & Row, 1965), 71.

31. Wikipedia. "Who Are You (The Who song)." Wikipedia. July 27, 2022. https://en.wikipedia.org/wiki/Who_Are_You_(The_Who_song).

32. Parker Palmer, *The Courage to Teach: Exploring the Inner Landscape of a Teacher's Life*, 10th Anniversary Edition (New York: John Wiley & Sons, 2017), 2.

33. Palmer, *The Courage to Teach: Exploring the Inner Landscape of a Teacher's Life*, 10.

34. Ken Wilber, *Integral Spirituality: A Startling New Role for Religion in the Modern and Postmodern World* (Boston: Shambhala Publications, 2006), 153.

35. Paulo Freire, *Pedagogy of the Oppressed* (New York: Continuum, 2006), 72, 75, 80.

36. Kessler, "The Teaching Presence," 11.

37. Genoud, "On the Cultivation of Presence in Buddhist Meditation."

38. Hanh, *Awakening of the Heart: Essential Buddhist Sutras and Commentaries*.

39. Thomas Keating, *Invitation to Love: The Way of Christian Contemplation*, 20th Anniversary Edition (New York: Bloomsbury, 2012); Ken Wilber, *Integral Spirituality: A Startling New Role for Religion in the Modern and Postmodern World* (Boston: Shambhala Publications, 2006); Ken Wilber, *The Religion of Tomorrow: A Vision for the Future of the Great Traditions—More Inclusive, More Comprehensive, More Complete* (Boston: Shambhala Publications, 2017).

40. Hanh, *Awakening of the Heart: Essential Buddhist Sutras and Commentaries*.

41. Reginald Ray, *Touching Enlightenment: Finding Realization in the Body* (Louisville, CO: Sounds True, 2008), xv.

42. Ibid., xvii.
43. David Abram, *The Spell of the Sensuous: Perception and Language in a More-Than-Human World* (New York: Vintage, 1996).
44. Abram, *Spell of the Sensuous*, 39.
45. Ray, *Touching Enlightenment*, 24–25.
46. Vicki Kelly, "A Métis Manifesto," in *A Heart of Wisdom: Life Writing as Empathetic Inquiry*, eds. Cynthia Chambers, Erika Hasebe-Ludt, Carl Leggo, and Anita Sinner (New York: Peter Lang, 2012), 364.
47. Richard Wagamese, *Embers: One Ojibway's Meditations* (Vancouver: Douglas & McIntyre, 2016), 30.
48. Wagamese, *Embers*, 36.
49. Buber, *I and Thou*, 23.
50. O'Reilley, *Radical Presence: Teaching as Contemplative Practice*, 9.
51. Mayes, "The Use of Contemplative Practices in Teacher Education," 21.
52. Coleman Barks, *The Essential Rumi* (New York: Castle Books, 1995), 7.
53. David Forbes, *Mindfulness and its Discontents: Education, Self, and Social Transformation* (Halifax, Nova Scotia: Fernwood Publishing, 2019), 6.

BIBLIOGRAPHY

Abram, David. *The Spell of the Sensuous: Perception and Language in a More-than-Human World*. New York: Vintage, 1996.
Aoki, Ted. "Layered Voices of Teaching: The Uncannily Correct and the Elusively True." In *Understanding Curriculum as Phenomenological and Deconstructed Text*, edited by William Pinar and William Reynolds, 17–28. New York: Teachers College Press, 1992.
Barks, Coleman. *The Essential Rumi*. New York: Castle Books, 1995.
Bennis, Warren, and Burt Nanus. *Leaders: The Strategies for Taking Charge*. New York: Harper & Row, 1985.
Buber, Martin. *The Knowledge of Man: Selected Essays*, edited and translated by Ronald Smith and Maurice Friedman. New York: Harper & Row, 1965.
———. *I and Thou*, translated by Ronald Smith. New York: Scribner, 2000.
———. *Between Man and Man*, translated by Ronald Smith. London: Routledge, 2002.
Cohen, Avraham. *Gateway to the Dao-Feld: Essays for the Awakening Educator*. Amherst, NY: Cambria Press, 2009.
Emerson, Ralph Waldo. *Poetry and Imagination*. Boston: James R. Osgood and Co., 1876.
Forbes, David. *Mindfulness and its Discontents: Education, Self, and Social Transformation*. Halifax, Nova Scotia: Fernwood Publishing, 2019.
Freire, Paulo. *Pedagogy of the Oppressed*. New York: Continuum, 2006.
Genoud, Charles. "On the Cultivation of Presence in Buddhist Meditation." *Journal of Consciousness Studies* 16, nos.10–11 (2009): 117–28.

Gethin, Rupert. *The Foundations of Buddhism*. Oxford: Oxford University Press, 1998.

Gunnlaugson, Olen, Charles Scott, Heesoon Bai, Ed Sarath, eds. *The Intersubjective Turn: Theoretical Approaches to Contemplative Learning and Inquiry Across Disciplines*. Albany: SUNY Press, 2017.

———. *Catalyzing the Field: Second-Person Approaches to Contemplative Learning and Inquiry*. Albany: SUNY Press, 2019.

Hadar, Linor, Oren Ergas, Bracha Alpert, and Tamar Ariav. "Rethinking Teacher Education in a VUCA World: Student Teachers' Social-Emotional Competencies during the Covid-19 Crisis." *European Journal of Teacher Education* 43, no. 4 (2020): 573–86.

Hanh, Thich Nhat. *Beyond the Self: Teachings on the Middle Way*. Berkeley, CA: Parallax Press, 2009.

———. *Awakening of the Heart: Essential Buddhist Sutras and Commentaries*. Berkeley, CA: Parallax Press, 2012.

Keating, Thomas. *Invitation to Love: The Way of Christian Contemplation*. 20th Anniversary Edition. New York: Bloomsbury, 2012.

Kelly, Vicki. "A Métis Manifesto." In *A Heart of Wisdom: Life Writing as Empathetic Inquiry*, edited by Cynthia Chambers, Erika Hasebe-Ludt, Carl Leggo, and Anita Sinner, 363–68. New York: Peter Lang, 2012.

Kessler, Rachel. "The Teaching Presence." *Holistic Education Review* 4, no.4 (1991): 4–15.

LeBlanc, Paul. "Higher Education in a VUCA World." *Change: The Magazine of Higher Learning* 50, nos. 3–4 (2018), 23–26.

Mayes, Clifford. "The Use of Contemplative Practices in Teacher Education." *Encounter: Education for Meaning and Social Justice* 11, no. 3 (1998): 17–31.

Miller, John. *The Contemplative Practitioner: Meditation in Education and the Workplace*, 2nd ed. Toronto: University of Toronto Press, 2014.

O'Donahue, John. *Eternal Echoes: Exploring Our Yearning to Belong*. New York: HarperCollins, 1999.

O'Reilley, Mary. *Radical Presence: Teaching as Contemplative Practice*. Portsmouth, NH: Boynton/Cook Publishers, 1998.

Palmer, Parker. *The Courage to Teach: Exploring the Inner Landscape of a Teacher's Life*, 10th Anniversary Edition. New York: John Wiley & Sons, 2017.

Ray, Reginald. *Touching Enlightenment: Finding Realization in the Body*. Louisville, CO: Sounds True, 2008.

Scott, Charles. "Hanging Out: One of the High Arts of Dialogue," *SFU Educational Review* 3 (2009). https://doi.org/10.21810/sfuer.v3i.343.

Senge, Peter, Otto Scharmer, Joseph Jaworski, and Betty Flowers. *Presence: An Exploration of Profound Change in People, Organizations, and Society*. New York: Currency, 2005.

Townshend, Pete. "See Me, Feel Me." *Tommy*. Decca/Track Records, 1969.

Wagamese, Richard. *Embers: One Ojibway's Meditations*. Vancouver: Douglas & McIntyre, 2016.

Wikipedia. "Who Are You" (The Who song)." July 27, 2022. https://en.wikipedia.org/wiki/Who_Are_You_(The_Who_song)

Wilber, Ken. *Integral Spirituality: A Startling New Role for Religion in the Modern and Postmodern World*. Boston: Shambhala Publications, 2006.

———. *The Religion of Tomorrow: A Vision for the Future of the Great Traditions—More Inclusive, More Comprehensive, More Complete*. Boston: Shambhala Publications, 2017.

Epilogue

The editors of this volume hail from diverse disciplinary and institutional backgrounds, as well as different levels of expertise in both online and contemplative pedagogies. Our home disciplines include education, social work, political science, and history. Two of us teach underserved undergraduates in small colleges, one works at a large, urban comprehensive university, and the last is affiliated with a fully online "open" postsecondary institution. We also come to contemplative pedagogy through personal practices that are rooted in different traditions and/or secular trainings: yoga, Shambhala, mindfulness-based stress reduction, Vipassana, the Plum Village tradition, and others. The idea for the book emerged out of monthly conversations about contemplative pedagogy that we have kept up since meeting each other in August 2018 at a summer institute on contemplative practices in education hosted by the Center for Contemplative Mind in Society. Each month, we have met virtually to discuss our own efforts to integrate contemplative methods into our postsecondary teaching, sharing high and low points, offering each other advice, and considering how our approaches intersected with broader debates in the field.

Inevitably, these exchanges took a different turn once the COVID-19 lockdowns forced universities around the world into emergency remote teaching. Since one member of the group had years of expertise in online education, they were able to help the other three to navigate the immense challenges of moving their face-to-face teaching online. Along the way, we commiserated about the immense workload and stress we were facing, and we kept returning to the problem of how to sustain our commitment to contemplative pedagogy in these exceptional circumstances. At the same time, the multiplying crises afflicting the world only strengthened our commitment to an education that fosters meaning and connection. We knew that other scholars and teachers rooted in the worlds of contemplative and online education must have developed their own insights into the challenge of sustaining presence in online learning communities during COVID-19. We decided to open up the conversation by hosting an online colloquium in May 2021, which in turn led to this current volume.

We acknowledge that the writings collected here represent just the beginning of a long road toward developing a contemplative pedagogy of online presence. In bringing together scholars and educators respectively in online education and in contemplative pedagogy, we observe differences in understandings and approaches to the concept of presence in online teaching and learning. As we tried to arrive at a common language of presence in teaching and learning, we recognized that while the online educators pointed to dimensions of presence in their everyday pedagogical practice *online*, some contemplative educators emphasized the significance of *offline* contemplative practices to support their students' online presence.

Contemplative pedagogy trailblazers Heesoon Bai, Charles Scott, and Laurie Anderson remind us that we are hardwired for presence as humans, and all contributors to this volume agree that presence is essential to successful and meaningful teaching and learning, whether online or in person. We joined in our shared purpose of bringing the whole person into a holistic teaching and learning space, as well as our vision of presence as always relational in our connection and attunement with the self, each other, and the collective and larger existence. We agree that presence is attainable yet challenged in different ways in the online and offline spaces. It might show up differently in distinctive offline and online conditions and contexts. Both learning spaces are nonetheless part of the online education environment. The main difference, however, is that online learning resources, events, and interactions are mediated by digital technology, which requires consideration of our relationship and habits related to technology. The question that remains to be addressed in greater depth is how we can foster contemplative presence in technology-moderated digital spaces. How can contemplative pedagogical practices promote meaningful and transformative learning with the help of digital technologies despite their potential harms?

With the exponential growth of the attention economy over the past decade, we can no longer ignore the current technology landscape that is driven by capitalist structures of competition and profit and characterized by persuasive technology designed to direct our attention, emotions, mindsets, and even values. Digital technology now exceeds not only human capabilities through artificial intelligence but also exploits human vulnerabilities with persuasive technologies to influence our thoughts and behaviors. In his critical writing about the attention economy, Peter Doran urgently reminds us how the "corporate capture of our mental faculties and attention in the service of a state-based ideology of endless economic growth" has got "under our skin and attempts to redefine the most intimate relationship of all: our relationship with ourselves and our sense of purpose and meaning."[1] It has become more important than ever to design online learning practices and create learning spaces to mitigate such harmful effects while harnessing the benefits of accessibility and connection to others and to information and knowledge across physical distance.

This volume highlights some affinities between contemplative and online learning approaches that can encourage the kind of holistic presence that both students and teachers need in this increasingly complex world. We can, for example, become more aware of our emotional responses/reactions to technology and the technological changes seemingly being forced upon us, and then respond from a place that is rooted in our values rather than our reactions. We can hone our skills in connecting with ourselves and others at a deep human level and we can bring those skills and capacities into all kinds of learning spaces. We can deepen our connection with the natural world around us, even through technology, and have that connection shape our ethical response to the world. We can create healthy habits of mind, so we are prepared to use technology with wise discernment. In cultivating our awareness—emotionally, spiritually, physically, socially, intellectually—we can strengthen our capacity for navigating—and shaping—the online world in a way that is grounded in compassion, the insight of interbeing, and the intrinsic value of all lives. In this collection of writings, we can see that it is indeed possible to engage the soul in learning in online spaces, but we have only just begun to map the way forward.

Further dialogue and collaboration between online educators and contemplative educators can strengthen the theory and practice of presence in ways that will enhance students' awareness and connection to their deeper purpose, helping them to avoid being driven by the angst of the ego in the fractured digital world. Our calling and commitment as educators require us to cultivate students' presence to the interdependence and relationality of their being in our shared human conditions, to make the right choices in their digital usage and habits for well-being, and to re-center their attention on the common good. We hope that our readers use this collection as a springboard to continue this exploration.

NOTE

1. Peter Doran, *A Political Economy of Attention, Mindfulness and Consumerism: Reclaiming the Mindful Commons* (London: Routledge, 2017), 16, doi:10.4324/9781315794075.

BIBLIOGRAPHY

Doran, Peter. *A Political Economy of Attention, Mindfulness and Consumerism: Reclaiming the Mindful Commons.* London: Routledge, 2017. doi:10.4324/9781315794075.

Index

(Page references for figures are italicized.)

Attention, xiv; xvi, xviii, 3, 15, 19, 20, 38, *39*, *42*; bare, 96; challenges to, xii; and empathy, 57; and mindfulness, 6, 41; and presence, viii, xii, 6, 16, 19, 22, 32; and online learning, 13, 22; teaching and, 51, 52, 122
attention economy, xii, 132
attentional literacy, 6, 7

body, xiv, *9*, 93, 98, *103–4*, 111, 115, 122, 125; in contemplative practice, 119; felt sense of, xiv, xvi, 2–3, 20, 57, 60, *76*, 95, 106n21; as a foundation of mindfulness, 96; movement and, 21, 56–57, 88. *See also* body scan, embodiment, mind-body-spirit connection, walking
body scan, 11, 19, 58, 95, 104n3
Buber, Martin, xvii, 85n2, 112, 116–17, 120

CMind. *See* Center for Contemplative Mind in Society.
Center for Contemplative Mind in Society (CMind), xv, 60, 79, 131

Community of Inquiry (CoI) xiii, xix, 29–43, 102, 118
compassion, xvii, 6, 15, 22, 61, 74–75, 81, 117, 133; practices of, 10, 57, 58, 71; and presence, 74–75; students' experience of, 15, 71; and teaching, 61, 63. *See also* self-compassion

digital disarray, xii, xivn23, 10, 19–20, 23n15, 45n35
digital well-being/wellness, 10, 11, 139
discussion boards, 15–16, 18, 29, *39*, *40*, 87, 89, 123

embodiment, xviii, 59–60, 94–95, 97–98, 100; and learning, 5, 55, 100, 121; practices of, xx, xxi, 94; and presence, xiv, xx, 94, 36, 95, 113, 119–21; and teaching, 102, 122. *See also* body; mind-body-spirit connection
emergency remote teaching, vii, ix, xi, xii, xviii, xix, xx, 56, 82, 131; difference with online teaching, ix, xi, xxiiin16; experience of, xi–xii, 61–62, 69, 73–74

emotions, 9, 18, 29, 37, 56, 57, 58, 63, 82, 119; and Community of Inquiry framework, 32, 35–36, 37; and learning, 6, 19, 30, 34, 35–36, 41; paying attention to, xvii, 2, *12*, 19; and persuasive technology, 132; and teaching, 6, 15
ethics, xvii, 2, 60, 77, 94, 95, 98, 133. *See also* ethical relations; social justice

free-writing, xv, 97. *See also* journals

grading, 83–84, 89, 97

holistic learning. *See* wholeness
hooks, bell, 75, 102, 103

indigenous knowledge/approaches, xv, 1, 2, 14–15, 33, 98, 111, 120
interbeing, xvii, xviii, xxviin62, 94, 98, 102, 115–16, 133
journals, 18, 19, 29, 70, 83, 84, 98. *See also* free writing

Kabat-Zinn, Jon, 3, 4, 6, 41, 58, 105n9

marking. *See* grading
mind-body-spirit connection, 5, 17, 20
mindfulness, xv, xvii, xix, xx, 1, 2, 3, 6, 56, 59, 60, 61, 63, 76, 98, 99, 103, 124; and Community of Inquiry approaches, 30, *33,* 34; definitions of, 6, 35, 41, 94; four establishments of, 96; in online learning, 6–7; practices of, 37, 40, *42,* 57, 58, 70, 95–96, 102, *104,* 118–19; and racial justice, 107n26

nature, xv, xx, 20, 78–79, 84, 87–90, 104, 120

Palmer, Parker, vii, 6, 79, 117

self-compassion, xx, 75, 76, 77
senses, xx, 8, 78, 79, 81, 88–89, 96, 114, 120
sensory, 56, 87–90, 96, 97, 98, 100, 114
silence, xx, 6, *11–12*, 16,18, 69–72, 111, 121
social justice, xvi, xx, 60, 65, 77, 94, 95, 98, 99, 101. *See also* ethics

teaching presence, xiv, xix, 39, 41, 52, 58–59, 114, 115, 120, 123; Community of Inquiry understandings of, xiii, 30, 31, 32, 35; differences with teach*er* presence, xix, 49, 51
Thich Nhat Hahn, xxviin62, 59–60, 94, 95, 102, 115–16, 118–19. *See also* interbeing.
trauma-informed approaches, 64, 77, 95

vulnerability, viii, xv, 8, 30, 37, 39, 55, 65, 69, 84; and connection, 14–15, 75, 102–3; space for, xvii, xx, xxi, 8, 39, 93–94, 102, 103; and teachers, xv, xx, 15, 39, 55, 61, 63, 65, 117

walking, xv, 59, 70, 78–79, *81*, 84; as mindfulness practice, 78–79, 88–90, 95–98, 99, 102
walking-based pedagogy, xx, 94–95, 97–98, 103
wholeness, xv, xvi, 5–6, 103
writing. *See* journals, free-writing

About the Authors

Laurie Anderson is the executive director of Simon Fraser University, Vancouver. He is also an adjunct professor in the Faculty of Education, an associate at SFU's Centre for Dialogue, and the codeveloper of SFU's popular master's program in contemplative inquiry and approaches in education. Before coming to SFU, he spent thirty years in the public education system, as a teacher, principal, director of curriculum, associate superintendent, and interim superintendent of schools for the Vancouver Board of Education. He has held various consultancy positions over the past twenty years, including on program reform strategies for the British Columbia Ministry of Education; assessment and evaluation frameworks for the Education Bureau of Hong Kong; facilitating leadership development and student evaluation programs in China, Thailand, Chile, Cambodia, Mexico, Vietnam, and Taiwan; and mentoring novice school leaders throughout British Columbia.

Heesoon Bai is a professor in the Faculty of Education at Simon Fraser University. She is a co-coordinator in the master's program in contemplative inquiry and approaches in education. Following Raimon Panikkar's (1918–2010) lead, she understands philosophy's task for today's troubled world to be "to know, to love, and to heal." She brings this threefold task of philosophy into her teaching and research. Her current research interests cluster around examining and deconstructing ontological and epistemological assumptions that underlie our cultural practices, our ethics, and our aesthetics. In her work she calls for reanimation of our selves within all spheres of human beingness in the service of living ethically and in beauty. Ethics and aesthetics are one. Through contemplative inquiry and practices, such as Zen, she offers ways to experiment with replenishing, nourishing, and animating our being.

About the Authors

Martha Cleveland-Innes is a professor of open, digital, and distance education at Athabasca University. She is the editor in chief of the bilingual *Canadian Journal of Learning and Technology* and the author of *The Guide to Blended Learning*. Martha is instructor, co-designer, and researcher for the open online courses Blended Learning Practice and Leading Change for Teaching and Learning in a Digital World. The second edition of *Introduction to Distance Education: Teaching and Learning in a New Era*, which she coedited, was released in 2021. In 2019 Martha received an honorary doctorate from Mid-Sweden University and the Leadership Award from the Canadian Network for Innovation in Education. She is currently a member of the Advisory Group for Digital Literacy with the British Columbia Ministry of Advanced Education, visiting professor of pedagogy at Mid-Sweden University, and virtual educator in residence, National University of Singapore.

Bill Cohen is a member of Nkmaplqs/Okanagan Indian Band with extensive kinship ties to Syilx Okanagan, Nlaka'pamux, and First Peoples throughout British Columbia and Washington. He is an artist and assistant professor in the University of British Columbia Okanagan School of Education. The focus of Bill's continuing research is to identify, understand, and theorize the transforming potential of Syilx Okanagan and Indigenous knowledge and pedagogy through organic language and cultural knowledge revitalization.

Deborah Dell holds a master's in counseling psychology and education and recently completed her doctorate in the distance education program at Athabasca University. Deborah has had a long career in the field of "unlearning," specifically through work involving untangling cognition and emotion to improve holistic health. More recently her work involves designing and developing workforce development and training for the addictions and mental health workforce, using in-person, online, and blended-learning modalities.

Leslie Ann Jeffrey is a professor of political science at the University of New Brunswick Saint John. She has been teaching international relations and comparative politics for over twenty-five years. She specializes in human rights, gender politics, and Global North/South relations. Her research interest in recent years has been on the role of contemplative practices in reconnecting students to themselves and the political, social, and environmental worlds around them.

Agnieszka (Aga) Palalas is an associate professor of open, digital, and distance education (ODDE) at Athabasca University and director of the MEd and EdD programs. Drawing from over twenty-five years of experience as a face-to-face and online educator, instructional designer, and an IT programmer, combined with her two-decade-long mindfulness practice, her scholarly interests lie in the area of mindfulness in online learning, digital well-being, and contemplative pedagogy and instructional design.

Karen Ragoonaden is the associate dean of teacher education in the Faculty of Education at the University of British Columbia. As the recipient of a Killam Prize and Tri-Council grants in social sciences and humanities, her research and publications focus on culturally sustainable pedagogy and well-being in relation to equity, diversity, and inclusion. Her publications and research interests lie in the area of mindfulness and well-being, culturally responsive pedagogy, and conceptions of teaching and learning. As a qualified yoga instructor, the concept of mindful educational practices is an integral component of her research and her practice.

Karen Robert is an associate professor of history at St. Thomas University, where she teaches courses on Latin American history, world history, research methods, and global automobility. A historian of modern Argentina, her work uses material culture to explore social history and cultural myths. Her current research examines labor politics, human rights, and memory through a history of the Ford Falcon, the automobile that came to symbolize state terrorism in contemporary Argentina. In 2023 she was appointed founding director of the history department's Institute of World History, which is currently in development. Dr. Robert's long-standing interest in innovative pedagogy has also led her to explore the use of mindfulness practices to deepen students' historical consciousness and cognitive skills. She has experimented with mindfulness approaches to teaching for several years, and served as remote teaching coordinator on her campus during the COVID-19 lockdown.

Charles Scott is an adjunct professor in the Faculty of Education at Simon Fraser University where he is co-coordinator of and teaches in a master's program in contemplative inquiry and approaches in education. He is also an associate professor at City University in Canada, where he was the former coordinator and instructor in the MEd leadership in education program; at City University, he has also taught courses in the MEd school counseling program and the MA of counseling program. His research interests are in contemplative inquiry, spirituality in education, dialogue in education, holistic education, and the considerations and intersections of curriculum, pedagogy, and assessment.

Margaret Anne Smith is an educator, poet, and fiber artist with a varied career as a teacher of American and environmental literature, a faculty developer, and a leader in arts education. She has taught numerous courses in literature at the University of New Brunswick and St. Stephen University.

Monika Stelzl is a professor at St. Thomas University. Her research interests include the examination of the construction of sexuality knowledge, women's accounts of sexual pleasure, and human-nature connection. She regularly teaches courses in the areas of human sexuality and human-nature connection. She is also a certified forest therapy guide.

Yuk-Lin Renita Wong is a professor at the School of Social Work at York University. Her scholarship and teaching aim to deconstruct the power relations in the knowledge production and discursive practices of social work, as well as re-centering marginalized voices and ways of knowing and being. She brings contemplative pedagogy into critical social work education and advances mindfulness as a decolonial embodied pedagogy and critical reflective practice in social justice work. Her coedited book, *Sharing Breath: Embodied Learning and Decolonization* (2018), engages with decolonization, embodiment, and critical studies in education. She has been a mindfulness practitioner since 1998 and leads meditation and mindfulness training in the tradition of Thich Nhat Hanh.

www.ingramcontent.com/pod-product-compliance
Lightning Source LLC
Chambersburg PA
CBHW030656230426
43665CB00011B/1115